LÉON BLUM

Léon Blum

Prime Minister, Socialist, Zionist

PIERRE BIRNBAUM

Translated by Arthur Goldhammer

Yale

UNIVERSITY

PRESS

New Haven and London

Frontispiece: Léon Blum, circa 1894

Yale University Press books may be purchased in quantity for educational, business, or promotional use. For information, please e-mail sales.press@yale.edu (U.S. office) or sales@yaleup.co.uk (U.K. office).

Set in Janson Oldstyle type by Integrated Publishing Solutions.
Printed in the United States of America.

Library of Congress Cataloging-in-Publication Data
Birnbaum, Pierre
Léon Blum : prime minister, socialist, Zionist / Pierre Birnbaum ; translated by Arthur Goldhammer.
pages   cm — (Jewish lives)
Includes bibliographical references and index.
ISBN 978-0-300-18980-3 (alk. paper)
1. Blum, Léon, 1872–1950. 2. Statesmen—France—Biography. 3. Socialists—France—Biography. 4. France—Politics and government—1914–1940. 5. Front populaire. I. Goldhammer, Arthur, translator. II. Title.
DC373.B5B57   2015
944.081'5092—dc23
[B]   2014039215

A catalogue record for this book is available from the British Library.

This paper meets the requirements of ANSI/NISO Z39.48-1992 (Permanence of Paper).

10 9 8 7 6 5 4 3 2 1

CONTENTS

LÉON BLUM

Introduction

JUNE 6, 1936, was a mild day in Paris. On that date the city celebrated the victory of the Popular Front. It was a turning point in French history: though threatened with virtual civil war, France had chosen to inaugurate a new era by granting the people a leading role in the public sphere. An elegant, self-assured individual rose to ask the Chamber of Deputies to grant him its confidence as France's new prime minister (*président du Conseil*). Léon Blum, the uncontested leader of the Socialist Party, took the podium and began to lay out his plans for the months ahead. He announced a number of key measures, including the forty-hour week, paid vacations, nationalization of certain firms, and steps to redistribute the nation's wealth. The atmosphere in the chamber was stormy, and tensions were running high. It was then that Xavier Vallat, the deputy from Ardèche, took the floor to make a statement that still commands our attention today: "Your accession to power, Mr. Prime Minister, is undeniably a historic date. For the first time, this old Gallo-Roman country will be governed . . . by a Jew." Ignoring the protests of the chair and the tumult in the chamber, Vallat continued: "I note that France will have for the first time its own Disraeli. . . . I say what I think . . . which is that in order to govern a peasant nation like France, it is better to have someone whose origins, modest though they may be, lie deep in the entrails of our soil, rather than a subtle Talmudist."[1]

Stunned by the vehemence of this attack before the representatives of the nation, Blum, pale with emotion, nevertheless "proudly" acknowledged his Judaism to his colleagues. He did so in the same terms he had used in an earlier debate in the Palais-Bourbon, in January 1923, concerning the occupation of the Ruhr, against which he had protested. On that occasion, after Léon Daudet interrupted him with an attack on "the Jewish bank" and Jean Ybarnégaray mocked him as a "Protestant Jew," Blum had replied: "From the [right-wing] benches I hear persistent repetition of the word 'Jew.' . . . I am a Jew. That is a fact. . . . You do me no injury by reminding me of the race to which I belong and have never renounced and toward which I feel only gratitude and pride."[2]

Although the chair now tried to silence Vallat by solemnly declaring that "I, for one, know neither Jews, as you call them, nor Protestants nor Catholics but only Frenchmen," irretrievable words had been spoken, words that would leave an indelible mark, foreshadowing the tragedy of Vichy to come. According to another transcript of Vallat's remarks, he even alleged that the "subtle Talmudist," the Jew without roots in French soil and the ominous new head of government, would decide France's foreign policy "only after consulting his co-religionists."[3] The nationalist right loudly applauded Vallat's speech, because in its view, "the government of Léon Blum puts the Jewish question before the French people for the first time since the Dreyfus Affair."[4] In other words, the nationalists urged French deputies and members of the Conseil Général of the Seine *département* to subscribe in 1936 to a barely updated version of *The Protocols of the Elders of Zion*, a notorious screed that had been all the rage in anti-Semitic circles for decades.[5]

Exactly thirty years after the end of the Dreyfus Affair (the captain's innocence had finally been acknowledged only in 1906), Léon Blum thus found himself the target of a comparable wave of anti-Semitic feeling, which attained its peak when he became prime minister in 1936. Cries of "Death to the Jews!" were heard several times within the Chamber of Deputies itself. This rising tide of anti-Semitism would lead directly to the tragedy of Vichy, followed by Blum's imprisonment in the fortress of Pourtalet, where, undaunted, he wrote: "We work *in* the present, not *for* the present." Commenting on this passage at a later date, Emmanuel Lévinas wrote: "1941! A hole in history. . . . A man in prison continues to believe in an unrevealed future. . . . To act in the name of remote ends while Hitlerism reigned triumphant . . . that, surely, is the height of nobility."[6]

The "man in prison," whose life was in constant danger, had only recently changed the course of French history with the Popular Front. For the first time, not only in France but in the modern era, a Jew who did not hide his identity but often proclaimed it with pride had become the head of a major government, a deep shock for many right-wing citizens, thus leading to a strong political anti-Semitic mobilization. Blum might have lacked roots in the soil, but he was by no means a "subtle Talmudist"; he cannot be compared to Disraeli either, who, though he never denied his origins, had converted to Anglicanism, or to Walter Rathenau, foreign minister of the Weimar Republic, "tormented" by his identity.[7] In this respect there truly is a French exception. As James Joll has remarked, "Blum and Rathenau . . . were both deeply influenced by the fact that they were Jews; and the difference in their attitudes to their Jewish heritage throws light both on their characters and on the position of the Jews in France and Germany. . . . Rathenau's death was directly due to the fact that he was a Jew; but it was not until the Germans had conquered and corrupted France that Blum's life was in danger for the same reason."[8]

Today, in the second decade of the twenty-first century, France remains exceptional in this regard: it is virtually the only country in the world, apart from Israel, that has several times chosen as its leader a Jew openly proclaiming his identity. Like Captain Dreyfus, who was allowed to enter the *sanctum sanctorum* of the French general staff, Léon Blum accepted a leading role in government, unleashing a powerful tidal wave of anti-Semitism. This moment in French history stands out, so much that an American anti-Semite hostile to the New Deal could declare: "The Jews and the Negroes run France. . . . America will not have a Léon Blum."[9] Meanwhile, far from the United States, in Turkey, Mustafa Kemal, the hero of the Turkish Republic, proclaimed that "in my view, democracy in today's France is degenerate. In any case, the French must someday revise their democratic system. This is a historical necessity. An extremist socialist like Léon Blum is the leader of this country even though he is neither French by race nor Catholic by religion. This cannot work."[10]

Hence no portrait of Léon Blum can ignore the essential fact of his Jewishness, which gave a specific coloration to his destiny: he was one of the many "state Jews" who took advantage of the universalistic and egalitarian values of the post-revolutionary French state, advancing through the meritocratic system to achieve emancipation through public service. In return these "state Jews" devoted themselves to serving the state as bureaucrats and civil servants and military officers, doing their utmost to protect and defend it. A product of France's most prestigious schools who spent much of his career as a high-ranking civil servant, Blum nevertheless joined the camp of social protest, and following the victory of the Socialist Party, his term as prime minister made him a new type of state Jew, for none had ever risen to the pinnacle of government office before. This man of uncommon talent tried to reconcile his Jewishness with his passion for government and his embrace of democratic norms. What follows is a portrait of *this* Léon Blum.

1

Portrait of a Young Jew

LÉON BLUM was born on April 9, 1872, to a Jewish family with deep roots in Alsace. His father, Abraham Blum, was born in Westhoffen, a small village near Strasbourg, while his mother hailed from Ribeauvillé in the Haut-Rhin *département.* This part of eastern France was the cradle of a deeply patriotic strain of French Judaism, which managed to preserve its distinctive traditions, customs, and social forms despite the universalistic orientation of French republicanism. Alsatian Jews continued to practice their religion, to intermarry, and to keep kosher while rapidly assimilating.[1]

In the 1840s, Abraham Blum, having changed his first name to Auguste, moved to Paris, where he went into business selling silk and ribbons and quickly prospered. Blum Frères, headed by Auguste and his two brothers Henri and Émile, grew rapidly until eventually it occupied three stories of a building on the Rue du Quatre-Septembre in the commercial district known as the Pletzl, the center of the Marais quarter, where many Jews lived. The family settled near the Boulevard Sébastopol not far from the Tour Saint-Jacques in the heart of this neighborhood, in which thousands of Jewish immigrants from Eastern Europe eventually made their homes.[2] Léon's birthplace was located on the Rue Saint-Denis, a major artery in this working-class and merchant quarter, far from the luxurious homes on the Plaine Monceau inhabited by the better-established and more assimilated Jewish bourgeoisie. His family was not among those that characterized themselves as "Israélites" rather than "Juifs"—a distinction intended to signify deep socialization in the dominant culture and toleration by the French aristocracy and *grande bourgeoisie*. Blum's family knew nothing of the salon culture described in Proust's *In Search of Lost Time*, in which elegant Israélites such as Charles Swann are received by the aristocratic Duke and Duchess of Guermantes.

Léon Blum began his education in various neighborhood schools before entering the Lycée Charlemagne in the heart of the Pletzl, far from the capital's noble lycées such as Condorcet and Janson de Sailly, where the Jewish bourgeoisie sent its children. His life seemed mapped out in advance, with ambitions similar to those of other Jewish merchants' offspring. But he did so well in school that he was admitted to Henri IV, the lycée favored by the intellectual elite. This marked a crucial turning point in his life, opening the door to the republican meritocracy. Still, young Léon held to tradition enough that he took kosher food with him to this temple of the intellect. In his diary for April 20, 1892, the lycée's proctor wrote that "Blum brought unleavened bread and meat prepared according to Jewish rites," a rare indication that young Léon kept faith with his Jewish identity even in the very public space of the lycée.[3]

As eager to assimilate as most other French Jews, Blum chose the royal road, passing the entrance exam for the École

Normale Supérieure in July 1890. This was the school most of the leading intellectuals of the day graduated from, as did a fair number of deputies. It was the most prestigious institution in the French university system, and those graduates who chose to enter public service were highly esteemed. In contrast to many other students, however, Blum did not conceal his private identity. To be sure, he subscribed to the rationalism of the Enlightenment, celebrated Victor Hugo's eightieth birthday with a delegation of other students, later attended the poet's funeral with yet another group of students, and also marched in the funeral procession of still another republican hero, Léon Gambetta. He was thus steeped in the powerful universalist symbolism of the Third Republic, whose glory was celebrated on these great national occasions.[4] Yet he remained a young Jew respectful of the values of the women who raised him: his mother and grandmother. At the time he wrote: "I was born to live in a bright, sunny country under a clear blue sky. This shows how much of my Semite blood has been preserved in its pure state. Honor me by acknowledging that it flows unmixed in my veins and that I am the untainted descendant of an unpolluted race." Although this vocabulary from another era may make us wince, it attests to young Léon's awareness that he sprang from a tightly knit milieu whose marriage and social customs preserved the Jewish community from outside influences. His grandmother, a bookseller who admired George Sand and embraced socialism, inculcated an ideal of justice. His mother, who also valued justice highly, was no less uncompromising when it came to preserving the integrity of traditional religious ritual. She kept kosher, lit sabbath candles, and made sure her sons said their prayers in Hebrew every night. Léon and his brothers all celebrated their bar mitzvahs, and the family gathered every year for Yom Kippur, Rosh Hashanah, and Passover.

In those days, many Jews from Alsace and Lorraine observed practices that tended to maintain tight ties among members of the community. In Lorraine, for example, the family of Émile Durkheim, the theorist of positivist sociology and *laïcité* (or strict secularism in the public sphere), celebrated the major religious holidays and married other Jews, thus preserving Jewish culture in a community also greatly influenced by the legacy of the Enlightenment.[5] Like Durkheim, who ceased to believe but continued to participate in religious rituals, wearing a suit to Yom Kippur eve services in Épinal, Blum also remained observant. To be sure, he wrote later: "I have never encountered people so utterly devoid of religious ideas or traditions. It is so bad that no one can say what Jewish dogma is. Among the people, the religion is nothing but a collection of traditional superstitions that are observed without any conviction, simply out of respect for the ancestors who performed these same rituals for twenty-five centuries. To the enlightened it no longer means anything."[6] Still, as is also the case with Durkheim and many other assimilated Jews, Blum's professed "respect" for Jewish tradition leaves us wondering how he answered his wife Lise Bloch when she said, "I suppose it doesn't matter to you that I will be traveling on Yom Kippur."[7] Like Durkheim and Salomon Reinach, Blum rejected the "superstitions" in Jewish dietary laws, which he ceased to observe as an adult, though he never denied being part of the Jewish diaspora.[8] "I, too, am rootless," he declared, presaging his 1940 declaration that "I am a wandering Jew."[9] Proof of his Jewishness can also be seen in his three marriages to Jewish women, the first of which was formally celebrated in the Grand Synagogue of Paris on the Rue de la Victoire, where Captain Dreyfus's marriage had been celebrated a short time before.

In most photographs from that time he appears as a languid, effeminate dandy preoccupied with the elegance of his attire, his hat, his monocle, and his gloves as well as with the grace of his movements and pose—the portrait of a young Jewish artist whose slightly bohemian "presentation of self" denies any virtue to strength.[10] This self-image was clearly one that Blum sought deliberately to project, since it is repeated in photograph after photograph. It differed in every way from the self-image that many high civil servants and high-ranking military officers aimed to create with their severe posture, rigid and austere attire, and stern, manly attitude—all intended to send a clear message of masculinity. The photograph of Blum in the first volume of his complete works, for instance, deliberately displays his "delicate and soft appearance, more fantastic than romantic, slightly stooped, with half-parted lips that inevitably remind us of his elder [Maurice] Barrès and his contemporaries [André] Gide and above all [Marcel] Proust," wrote Colette Audry.[11] The self-portrait Blum sought to paint from one image to the next was more that of an artist than of a young civil servant. In terms of deep psychology, he apparently wished to portray himself as completely different from the typical French "state Jew." A skilled dancer, "little Bob," as his friends called him, was the life of the ballroom, and his svelte figure appealed to the many pretty women drawn to his elegance, grace, and dandyish manner.

This image of Léon Blum apparently stands in sharp contrast to that of Alfred Dreyfus, the prototype of the rigid state Jew in his starched uniform, stoically bearing up under an unending barrage of insults and injuries. Dreyfus presented himself as a disciplined officer eager to conform to military regulation in every detail; he was a silent, dignified hero, a prisoner who bore his lengthy torture without protest, and a distinguished, courageous soldier who, once exonerated of his alleged crimes, silently rejoined the ranks on the battlefield during the Great War. While Dreyfus's enemies caricatured his nature, deformed his features, depicted him as an animal, and ridiculed him mercilessly, many drawings portrayed the unfortunate captain as the starchy soldier he sought to embody.

Blum himself fully grasped the contrast between his own persona and that of Dreyfus when he wrote: "Dreyfus appeared in Rennes in person, grave, severe, modest, physically incapable of the slightest theatrical gesture or accent, but moving by dint of stoic purity."[12] A starker contrast between two men can hardly be imagined.

At first glance, these two state Jews thus seem different in every way. Whether as a young student at the École Normale Supérieure or later as leader of the Popular Front, Léon Blum struck a Proustian pose as a man intimate with literary circles and high society, a cultivated aesthete skipping lightly from one literary magazine to another, trying his hand at poetry, often attending the theater, and engaging in literary rather than martial jousts as a critic who rubbed shoulders with the elite. Dreyfus and Blum could hardly have chosen more different self-images.[13]

Yet at the time of the Dreyfus Affair, Blum was in fact a member of the Council of State, the highest administrative law court in France. He was a jurist whose bold and uncompromising interpretations of the law proved invaluable to Fernand Labori, the lawyer representing Émile Zola, who had only recently come with great fanfare to Dreyfus's defense. Indeed, if we look at Blum and Dreyfus from the proper angle, the two men actually appear quite similar. Although Dreyfus was born in 1859 and belonged to the generation that had experienced the trauma of the Franco-Prussian War and the loss of Alsace and Lorraine to the Germans, while Blum was not born until after the war, in 1872, their social backgrounds were quite comparable. Both sprang from a Jewish subculture that was at once traditional, emancipated, and patriotic, endogamic (that is, likely to marry within the group) and assimilated—a Jewish bourgeoisie that gradually abandoned its usual economic activities to pursue careers in government service. Both attended prestigious schools before going to work for the state: Dreyfus was a graduate of the École Polytechnique, and Blum attended the École Normale Supérieure.

In spite of these similarities and a broadly shared social imagination, there were many differences, too. Dreyfus took care to affirm the virile side of his personality and was perceived as masculine by his contemporaries, while Blum apparently took pleasure in constructing an image of himself as a dandy concerned above all with striking an elegant figure, a man who spoke in tones so low that he was scarcely audible. To his many enemies he thus came to symbolize the eternally fragile Jew, incapable of standing up to force—a weak, whining, elusive individual. His self-presentation seems to have encouraged anti-Semitic pamphleteers to describe him as the precise opposite of Dreyfus: an effeminate personality instead of a manly one. There are many examples of newspaper articles, caricatures, and songs from the 1930s attacking Blum's allegedly ambiguous sexuality. Gustave Téry, for instance, commented that Blum "was deeply marked by the influence of women. . . . At the École Normale he is remembered mainly as an overly delicate ephebe with wavy hair and wiggling hips. . . . The Israélite boy-child was fond of sitting on his classmates' laps and of being hugged in the Greek manner."[14] For Téry, the mere sight of Blum was enough to reveal "his coyness, his inappropriate humor, his limp gestures, his unmanly appearance, his exaggerated lamentations. . . . All of this was perfectly in keeping with the tearoom revolutionary, the cult of the gratuitous act, and the classical verse penned in 1893 by the twenty-year-old student 'in search of lost time.'"[15]

Jean-Pierre Maxence offers a similar view: "There was nothing virile in this pale shadow of a man. The voice was feminine; the gestures were feminine; the anxieties, the tearful rages, the oaths, the crises—here was an educated woman who cut a dazzling figure in her salon. In the heat of a political rally, she was the female who first stalks the male, sniffs him, flatters him, and then threatens him with her moans."[16] For Léon Daudet he was a "g-ggirl," a "mam'zelle," a "hybrid creature who rages and trembles like a woman, with oriental ferocity."[17] For Charles Maurras he was "the maiden" or "Bloom-Flower, baptized with the pruning knife." Henri Béraud called him "Blumish, a little woman prepared to scratch."[18] Pierre Gaxotte saw a "Palestinian filly, constantly whining, moaning, sniveling, wailing, twisting her handkerchief, wriggling, fainting."[19] *L'Action Française* portrayed Blum as "a grand hysteric, a madwoman ready for a straitjacket." The extreme left echoed the extreme right on this and other points. In 1925 *L'Humanité* pointed to the "Freudian squirming" of "a great coquette" who was in reality merely "an elderly retainer of the bourgeoisie."[20] Later, Maurice Thorez, the leader of the Communist Party and Blum's ally in the Popular Front before becoming his enemy again afterward, wrote that "Blum has stopped wriggling and squealing like the repugnant reptile he is. Lately he has been giving free rein to his savage instincts as a bourgeois exploiter."[21]

Bearing no resemblance whatsoever to Max Nordau's "muscle Jew," Blum's body easily fit the mold of anti-Semitic stereotypes. He was a Chagall rabbi, all wrapped up in himself: "As he spoke, he clasped in front of his chest his long, sensitive hands, the hands of a miracle-working rabbi, in a rather supplicating gesture that revealed both his tender heart and his eagerness to convince," wrote the actress and novelist Simone Le Bargy in her memoir. "The tenderness that was so abundantly evident to his friends was still more abundant when it came to suffering humanity."[22] For many, he was the image of the decadent Jew steeped in the arts, poetry, and literature. Even his friends referred to his supposed femininity: Jules Renard saw him as "graceful as Antigone . . . a beardless boy." His youthful friends Pierre Louÿs and André Gide described him as "Blum the ephebe." His manner was in many ways similar to that of

Marcel Proust, who had a Jewish mother and maintained a highly ambiguous attitude toward his Jewish identity, which many contemporaries associated with his homosexuality. Blum allegedly shared Proust's "wiles" and even his perversions, and many songs and poems alluded to his supposed homosexuality.[23] Proust was an aesthete often seen in high-society salons from which Blum, who came from a more modest social background, was on the whole excluded, although he was admitted to the salon of Geneviève Straus, which inspired Proust's description of the Guermantes salon. Their relations were far from cordial, and Proust in his correspondence made fun in several places of Blum's literary efforts, which he considered mediocre.[24] Still, a "mimetic rivalry" seems to have grown up between two writers who shared similar values and attitudes, and Proust called attention to the resemblance of some of their verses.[25] Some even argue that Blum was the first to write, in "Fragment on a Prayer," about the maternal goodnight kiss that would play a crucial role in Proust's *Search*.[26]

Effeminate dandy, poet, and art critic, the opposite of Alfred Dreyfus in every way, Blum thus seemed closer to Proust, because he saw himself as "a vulnerable and fragile being, 'like a girl in a novel,' he said, an overly delicate plant."[27] Like Proust, he nevertheless proved himself to be a decisive man who demonstrated manly courage, similar to that of Captain Dreyfus, with his impassive martial exterior. A great admirer of Stendhal, on whose work he was an acknowledged expert, Blum became, like the author of *Lucien Leuwen*, a member of the Council of State, where he displayed the courage of his hero and of his hero's characters Fabrice and Lucien, bold young men who repeatedly sought opportunities to prove their bravery in duels. In turn-of-the-century France, many insults were settled by duels, which provided an opportunity to demonstrate manliness in a public and incontrovertible way. Such displays of physical courage impressed not only adversaries but also the general public, which was compelled to concede the masculinity of any swashbuckler who braved the possibility of a serious wound or even death. Some forty duels were fought in connection with the Dreyfus Affair.

Even Proust, the delicate author of *In Search of Lost Time*, overcame his physical debilities long enough to defend his honor in several duels with sword and pistol. Both in connection with the Dreyfus Affair and in response to comments on his physique, he challenged those who insulted his honor. In 1920, for example, after *Sodom and Gomorrah* came out, he wrote to one of his critics: "You open the door to all sorts of nastiness when you call me 'feminine.' From 'feminine' to 'effeminate' is but a short step. The men who have served as my seconds in duels will tell you whether I have the softness of the effeminate."[28] Proust did not hide his readiness to confront his adversaries: "I had," he wrote, "a passion for dueling."[29] On another occasion, when a dispute broke out in a café, Proust felt he had been insulted: "I saw an opportunity for what I had once so loved, and which my health in no way prevented me from attempting again: a duel. But my friends insisted that it was out of the question, that I had nothing to do with their dispute, and that dispatching seconds would be ridiculous and unavailing."[30]

On October 14, 1912, Léon Blum fought a famous duel with theater critic Pierre Weber, which inevitably recalled Proust's earlier duel with critic Jean Lorrain. Journalists were present for the early morning confrontation, and a cameraman immortalized the scene in a short amateur film. The film shows Blum, as always elegantly attired for the occasion, in the broad-brimmed hat of a poet who has somehow wandered onto a battlefield, aggressively attacking his adversary with sword thrusts that might have proved fatal. The journalists on the scene all agreed: according to *L'Aurore*, on the third sally "M. Pierre Weber received a penetrating thrust to his right side, ending the fight. The wound was less serious than it seemed at first. The tip of the épée had been halted by [Weber's] rib, but had it been a centimeter higher, it might have been fatal, because it would have touched the liver. The adversaries did not reconcile."[31] Similarly, for *L'Intransigeant*, a newspaper that in the past had made no secret of its hostility to Dreyfusards and remained hostile to the values that Blum represented, "the combat was intense. . . . This was a serious duel that at several points came close to ending tragically. . . . M. Blum, a tall man with a fiery gaze behind his glasses . . . wore a black shirt, a black hat, and gray tennis shoes."[32] The description in *Le Temps* was even more detailed:

> Owing to the manner of M. Blum's attack, a certain anxiety gripped the spectators. . . . After a *seconde* parry and a *sixte* parry M. Blum made a powerful charge. . . . During the pause, M. Blum walked with M. Porto Riche. M. Weber sat. After two minutes, the duel resumed more vigorously than before. And suddenly, a moment of anxiety . . . M. Blum's épée grazed M. Weber's face. Another pause and another resumption. This time the adversaries seemed calmer and eyed each other warily. M. Blum tried to catch his opponent off-balance. At one point, the adversaries picked up the pace. M. Blum took an épée to the left hand, and blood flowed. Then came the dénouement: suddenly M. Blum was able to catch his adversary's blade . . . a direct thrust followed. M. Weber fell backward. The witnesses rushed forward, opened his shirt . . . a centimeter lower and the liver would have been hit. The wounded man was carried off. "A clean thrust ended a brawl," the master of ceremonies commented.[33]

This article leaves no doubt as to the violence of the confrontation. The front page of *L'Ouest-Éclair* called it "a ferocious duel. . . . M. Blum, who aimed at M. Weber's body, succeeded in hitting his sternum. A centimeter either way and the wound would have been fatal."[34] All the journalists insisted on the violence of the blow and on Blum's aggressiveness: he "attacked quite vigorously" and "charged" several times, the combat was "intense" and might have proved "fatal" or "tragic." In other words, despite his self-presentation as a dandy, a figure more often seen in society salons than fighting duels, Blum, like Dreyfus, was a man of undeniable physical courage, engaged in traditionally masculine pursuits.[35]

2

The Dreyfus Affair

LÉON BLUM — gentle poet, gifted writer, assimilated Jew, and successful socialite—was at first indifferent to the Dreyfus Affair, as he himself admits. In September 1897, his old mentor, Lucien Herr, the celebrated librarian of the École Normale, visited Blum at his country home and challenged him with a stark question: "Are you aware that Dreyfus is innocent?" Blum was dumbfounded. "Dreyfus?" he responded. "Who is Dreyfus? The captain had been arrested, convicted, stripped of his rank, and deported nearly three years earlier. . . . No one had given him a thought since then, and it took considerable effort to recall the events associated with his name. . . . Since that time, I had not given him a thought, and my conscience rested easy."[1]

During those three years, the fate of the man held prisoner on Devil's Island, wrongly accused of being a German spy, had been the last thing on Blum's mind. He acknowledged that he had behaved like most other Jews, who "did not want anyone to think that they were defending Dreyfus because Dreyfus was Jewish. . . . Indeed, they did not wish to feed anti-Semitic passions by rushing to the defense of another Jew." Blum himself, as a "typical Jew . . . unconsciously balancing family ties against everyday acquaintances, had no more pronounced vocation than anyone else to receive the Dreyfusard grace."[2] At first, he explained his lack of interest in Dreyfus as a consequence of moving among Jews who were afraid of being held hostage by the affair: "It would be a serious mistake to think that in the Jewish circles in which I traveled at that time—middle-class Jews, young men of letters, and civil servants—there was the slightest hint of pro-Dreyfus sentiment."[3]

At the time Blum was making a name for himself in the world of letters. He published in poetry magazines such as *La Conque* and *Le Banquet* and contributed many theater reviews to *Comedia* and *Le Matin*. Sophisticated Parisian society opened its doors to him, and he was much in demand. His criticism was feared; his articles were argued about and stirred polemics. In 1892 he joined the *Revue Blanche*, a literary magazine published by the Natanson brothers, to which he contributed many articles as in-house literary critic. He analyzed the works of Anatole France, Jules Renard, Pierre Louÿs, and André Gide and reviewed numerous foreign writers, including Edgar Allan Poe, Charles Dickens, Oscar Wilde, Leo Tolstoy, and Henrik Ibsen. He also commented frequently on the works of Jewish writers such as Marcel Schwob, Tristan Bernard, and Georges de Porto-Riche.[4] Some of his close friends even reproached him for attending too closely to the work of Jewish writers. André Gide confided to his diary:

> Thinking again tonight about Blum, to whom I cannot deny the qualities of nobility, generosity, and chivalry, although these words cannot be applied to him without distorting their true meaning, it seemed to me that his insistence on putting Jew

forever in the limelight, on focusing primarily on them, and his predisposition to see in them talent and even genius, stems first of all from the fact that a Jew is particularly sensitive to Jewish qualities, and above all from the fact that Blum believes the Jewish race to be superior, as though destined to dominate after having been dominated for so long, and that it is his duty to work for the triumph of his race, to assist it with all his might. In the rise of this race he no doubt sees the solution to many social and economic problems. . . . Why speak of flaws? For me it is enough that the qualities of the Jewish race are not French qualities. He thinks that the Jews' time will come. . . . He likes to give himself an air of importance. . . . He speaks to you only as your protector. At a dress rehearsal, in the corridors of a theater where he runs into you by chance, he puts his arm around your waist or neck or shoulders and even if you haven't seen him for a year makes you believe that you had last met only the day before and that he has no closer friend than you.[5]

Many of Blum's enemies also believed that he had a special taste for Jewish writers. The celebrated critic Émile Faguet, for instance, wrote: "M. Blum is in some ways a critic about whom people say, when a new play is announced, 'I know in advance what he will say about it. It's an ethnic matter.'"[6] The very influential *Revue Blanche*, whose contributors included Stéphane Mallarmé, Guillaume Apollinaire, and Charles Péguy, was considered "Jewish" by its adversaries. Léon Daudet, for instance, wrote that "when the Dreyfus Affair erupted . . . the Jews . . . possessed an unusual organ that was ethnically theirs, in which anarchy was tinged with literature and with biblical and political frenzy: the *Revue Blanche* of the brothers Natanson."[7] Indeed, there can be no doubt that among the magazine's contributors, Jewish bonds of sociability were strong.[8]

People close to Blum, many of whom belonged to the same literary circles, tried to alert him to the importance of the affair at the time of Dreyfus's arrest or shortly thereafter. Bernard

Lazare, who belonged to the *Revue Blanche* circle, was immediately convinced of Dreyfus's innocence and communicated his belief to Blum, who listened with a distracted ear. Lazare was of course one of the heroes of the affair, who fought courageously on the captain's behalf. The "first of the Dreyfusards," as Blum would later call him, was also in his eyes "a Jew of the noblest race, the prophetic race."[9] Lazare was aware that he played a leading role: "I want people to say that I was the first to speak, that the first person to stand up for the Jewish martyr was a Jew. . . . People must know that this Jew found friends among his own kind."[10] It was he who drafted the first pamphlet proving that Dreyfus was innocent and who moved heaven and earth to have the verdict overturned, challenging the powerful men at the heart of the unjust social order. His anarchist views drove him to act. As Blum recalled in 1935, Lazare's "morning visit should have troubled me; his conviction should have impressed me. Yet I listened to him with incredulous prejudice, like so many others, without really giving him my full attention."[11]

In retrospect, Blum saw clearly what had happened: "In order to appreciate the nature of 'the Affair' properly, you have to remember that Dreyfus was Jewish, that a Jew always remains a Jew, and that the Jewish race hereditarily suffers from certain blemishes! And was not one of those perpetually transmissible ethnic characteristics precisely an innate need to commit treason?"[12] The inherently Jewish aspect of the affair was suddenly blindingly obvious to him. To justify his own indifference, he accused middle-class and wealthy Jews like himself of having been afraid of undermining their status as assimilated Jews. He clearly forgot that, apart from Lazare, the captain's earliest defenders, from the very first days of the affair, were nearly all well-to-do Jews, including Dreyfus's brother Mathieu, his in-laws the Valabrègues, the Hadamards, Joseph, Salomon, and Théodore Reinach, Jules Isaac, Victor Basch, Lucien Lévy-Bruhl, and many others, who for a long time carried on the fight alone. It is therefore impossible to deny, as too many historians still do, the specifically Jewish aspect of their engagement. To be sure, these people fought on behalf of justice, human rights, and republican ideals, but it is not easy to distinguish the motivations of the abstract citizen from those of Jews who suddenly saw their community's place in the nation called into question. In this respect, the Dreyfus Affair and the anti-Semitism it aroused forced the intellectuals of the *Revue Blanche* to reevaluate the importance of their Jewish identity. Many assimilated Jews on the left became not only intellectuals but Jewish intellectuals.[13]

Because Blum devoted his energy to his literary career and to his social life and was, like so many others, reluctant to get involved in a conflict that might have compromised his status as an assimilated Jew, it took him a long time to understand the true nature of the Dreyfus Affair.[14] It was only after he was visited by Lucien Herr, the sage of the École Normale Supérieure, who had become his close friend, that Blum's view suddenly changed in the late summer of 1897. At that moment, his "mind was made up. As soon as vacation was over, we would restore the innocent man's good name and reveal to the country the name of the guilty party."[15] Like Marcel Proust and many other Jewish writers associated with the *Revue Blanche*, Blum had been slow to realize what was going on. But once he did, he offered his assistance to Fernand Labori, the attorney for Émile Zola, and to Georges Clemenceau, at that time the attorney for *L'Aurore*. Blum interpreted the law and even drafted for the defense briefs that revealed his considerable talent as a jurist; he attended several sessions of Zola's trial, signed petitions, solicited signatures, and even took part in street brawls. He went to see Maurice Barrès, his "teacher" and "guide," who "cared for [him] as an elder brother" but refused to sign the petition, having already joined the anti-Dreyfusard camp. Barrès's letter to him plunged him "almost into mourning." He became even more dejected a few days later, when Barrès published an article titled "The Protest of the Intellectuals," in which he attacked Zola, who "is not French," and denounced the "Jewish signers" who protested the condemnation of Dreyfus.

The poet Pierre Louÿs, who had been Blum's closest friend since their school days at Henri IV, also refused to sign, while Mallarmé sat on the sidelines. Blum felt he had no choice but to "distinguish among" his friends, thus leaving him even more deeply immersed in an intellectual circle composed largely of Jews, who joined the fight alongside such non-Jews as Anatole France, Charles Péguy, and Jean Jaurès, leading Protestants such as Gabriel Monod and Lucien Herr, renowned scientists such as Paul Langevin, the directors of the Institut Pasteur and the École Normale Supérieure, and many university professors. They drew support from certain salons frequented by the enlightened aristocracy, as Proust describes in his *Search*.

Opposition came from leading national and regional newspapers, which were by and large hostile to Dreyfus, from the army, from virtually every politician and jurist in the country, from the "patriotic leagues," from a considerable segment of the extreme left, and from immensely influential anti-Semitic pamphleteers such as Édouard Drumont, as well as a star-studded array of artists, including the painters Degas, Renoir, and Toulouse-Lautrec and writers Paul Valéry and above all Maurice Barrès. For Blum, Barrès, the prince of letters and his "elder brother," had chosen "national instinct" as his "rallying point," with "Boulangist solidarity" gaining the upper hand over what had once been the centerpiece of his oeuvre, namely, individual freedom: "the cult of the self." Barrès joined the reactionary bloc hostile to the Third Republic: "What unifies the conservative nationalist party is devotion to the Catholic religion."[16]

It was around this time that Blum wrote an important series of essays styled as "New Conversations of Goethe with

Eckermann," imaginary dialogues between Johann Wolfgang von Goethe and Johann Peter Eckermann, modeled after Eckermann's influential *Conversations with Goethe* (1836–1848). The essays appeared anonymously in *Revue Blanche* from 1897 to 1900, and then were published in book form in 1901. Using the rationalist Goethe as his mouthpiece, Blum ranged across many topics, and in one of these essays he dwelled at length on Barrès's recently published novel *Les déracinés* (The Uprooted), "a noteworthy book, the most important to have been published in France in quite some time." Although he greatly admired Barrès, he could not refrain from making one critical point:

> Barrès would have preferred to see these young men from Lorraine remain tied to their native soil, because he is a nationalist and a federalist. . . . But I wonder if Barrès, like Taine, has not attached too much importance to the influence of milieu, if he has not rather incautiously placed his faith in the soul of race and region. . . . Indeed, Barrès was once the theorist of the self and has remained to some extent an individualist, so I ask what has become of the self and the individual in his theory. Groups like the family and village sap the energy of the individual like nothing else. . . . What is just in this moment of humanity's history is what must be realized.[17]

Though previously torn between his friends, his work for the Council of State, and his sudden passionate involvement in the Dreyfus Affair, Blum finally took the plunge on February 15, 1898. He wrote to his friend André Gide, who at first evinced little enthusiasm for the Dreyfusard cause but was eventually won over by Blum's arguments: "No private concerns can prevail against the fever that has overtaken us. . . . I have given up all of my own work and still bitterly regret that my work for the Council along with the extraordinary tedium of the courtroom prevented me from returning after the first session of the trial."[18] He nevertheless took the precaution of signing his March 15, 1898, contribution to the *Revue Blanche* "A Jurist," thus preserving his anonymity. This was a carefully constructed piece whose systematic repetition of such phrases as "It is proven that" and "It is established that" was reminiscent of Zola's famous article "J'accuse." In it, Blum unambiguously identified himself as a high civil servant prepared to attack "the bad faith of the government and court." He added that "what must shock any judicial mind, indeed any fair-minded individual, is the dual role played in this affair by the Minister of War, who as plaintiff calls for proof but as minister prevents it from being produced." He denounced not only "the legal obstacles" but also the "extralegal" if not outright "illegal" ones as well as the "procedural artifices" placed in the way of Zola's defense.[19]

Three months later, on June 15, once again under the by-line "A Jurist," he published another article in the *Revue Blanche* in which he attacked the *lois scélérates*, or "villainous laws" restricting freedom of the press and the right to associate, which had been passed in the wake of anarchist attacks in 1894. In his view, these laws "endanger[ed] the fundamental freedoms of French citizens" and were "truly villainous laws of the Republic." Furthermore, they "reek of tyranny, barbarity, and lies. . . . To my mind, this ministry of the law of 1894 is also the ministry of the Dreyfus Affair. A truly admirable history! May I say that I did not await the Dreyfus Affair to conceive a hatred of brutality, to detest reaction, militarism, and authoritarianism, or to ask the republican government to respect the liberties of the Republic."[20]

Blum was by then a full-fledged state Jew, though he differed from other late-nineteenth-century state Jews in a number of respects: he was more willing to challenge the existing social order, more open to socialism, which many of his colleagues rejected, and more interested in poetry and in literary and social criticism, as evidenced by his writing for literary magazines such as *Le Banquet* and *La Revue Blanche* and by his book *Du mariage* (On Marriage, 1907), to which few other state Jews would have signed their names. He was nevertheless a state Jew who had followed the royal road of republican meritocracy, from the École Normale Supérieure to the Council of State, and who was even then turning over in his mind a veritable theory of the state. Paradoxically, however, as early as April 1899, and thus after his engagement in the Dreyfusard cause, we find Blum (again writing as Goethe) attacking Jewish functionaries (of whom he was one):

> These civilian and military functionaries chose their careers willingly, embraced them freely. Hence they must not be astonished when obliged to endure the consequences of their engagement. Which of them was unaware, upon entering public service, that he would be accepted or rejected by his comrades for reasons having nothing to do with personal merit? . . . Too many Jews hastened to take up government posts all at once. It is not a bad thing if they leave those posts now, even against their will. The role of the functionary was ill adapted to the fundamental nature of their race. They acquired the habit of curt contempt, of impeccable, concise dismissiveness, which others found repellent. The most gifted youths were selected for careers in public service, an absurd practice. The highest gifts of the intelligence are needed by merchants, manufacturers, and shopkeepers, by anyone pursuing a career in which the individual depends on himself alone and bears sole responsibility for his decisions; those gifts are of no use to the bureaucrat in civil or military service, where they may well prove harmful. . . . Let us therefore rejoice if young Jews are set back on their proper path, even if it is as a result of despicable actions and contemptible passions. Their true nature will be preserved. . . . They will find that they are freer and happier people.[21]

This fierce critique of his own professional background is surprising in a number of ways. Blum virtually dismisses republican meritocracy, which he sees as subject to ever-shifting political influences. More than that, he deplores the fact that Jews who have gone into government service have abandoned their intrinsic qualities and become contemptuous and dismissive in their dealings with the public. Functionaries like these would be likely to reject the ideas of a man like Bernard Lazare and dismiss their "religion of justice," as Blum himself did for many years. Blum (writing as Goethe) continues: "Insofar as I am able to make out the collective ambition of their race, it is leading them toward Revolution. The critical spirit is powerful in them."[22] A fresh convert to socialism, Blum at this point placed all his hope "among proletarians, clever craftsmen, and hard-working and generous youths among the petite bourgeoisie. That is where the sap is rising"—the revolutionary sap he found lacking among his co-religionists in government service.[23]

Blum's rather naive social determinism led him to underestimate the degree of reactionary and anti-Semitic sentiment in the very segments of society in which he placed his hopes. "Do not forget that the Semites are nearly all concentrated in big cities," he wrote. "Urban workers are not likely to be turned into fanatics by absurd fables, besides which they are much more suspicious of anti-Semites than of Jews." In his view, the origin of French anti-Semitism "is not in the lower classes but in high society. It is born in select circles and at the racetrack. What originates in such places will not spread very far."[24] Written in April 1899, at the height of what I have called "the anti-Semitic moment," which began in January 1898 and brought rabidly anti-Semitic mobs into the streets throughout France, Blum's optimistic remarks tell us a great deal about his ignorance of the threat posed by the anti-Semitic leagues that recruited among the lower classes and took part almost daily in violent clashes in the streets of Paris, including the very neighborhood where Blum resided.[25] With a convert's zeal for socialist ideals, he had no fear of "a Saint Bartholomew's Day of the Jews."[26] Such a thing might be possible "in Poland, Galicia, or Romania, or maybe in Algiers, but not in France. That's nothing but a manufactured sentiment."[27] He closed his eyes to the reality of anti-Semitism in France in the name of an idealized vision of the people.[28]

In 1899, after the Dreyfusard grace had descended upon him and alienated him somewhat from his duties as a high-ranking civil servant, Blum thus turned on his colleagues, whose ideas, which he had only recently shared, were allegedly at odds with true Jewish values—values of "justice" identified with "social revolution." Blum's conversion to Dreyfusism and socialism had led him, in other words, to unleash a fierce and unjust critique against the state and its servants, an attack on the republican bureaucracy, and a surprising protest against the French model of emancipation, under which the state used its power to bring Jews into high government posts and thus favor their upward mobility in society. Although it is true that many Jews who entered government service formed vertical alliances with those above them in the hierarchy (the traditional form of upward mobility in France), many of them nevertheless kept faith with their roots: like Dreyfus and Blum, they remained members of the Jewish community, married within it, and to one degree or another respected its traditions. In this sense, they honored the ancient principle of *dina de malkhuta dina*— the law of the country is the law—a dictum that takes on its full meaning in a strong state like France, which demands such loyalty and rewards it with career promotions for those with the requisite skills. Indeed, Blum's formula could be stood on its head: "the role of the functionary was well adapted to the fundamental characteristics of their race," which did not encourage the kind of social revolution to which Blum now aspired.

Later, after learning of Dreyfus's death on July 12, 1935, Blum published a series of articles in *Marianne*, a newspaper of the republican left, articles that were ultimately collected and published under the title *Souvenirs sur l'Affaire* (Memories of the Affair). Here, his criticism of Jewish functionaries focused less on their role in government than on their personal behavior. Instead of blaming them for turning their backs on social struggle and accepting government posts, he accused them of cowardice: "Jewish functionaries were afraid of joining the fight for Dreyfus, just as they are afraid today of joining the fight against fascism. Their only thought was to bury their heads in the sand and hide. They had no more idea then than they have now that no precaution or pose is likely to fool the enemy and that they themselves will be the first victims of the triumph of anti-Dreyfusism or fascism."[29] Invoking "memory" while ignoring historical reality, Blum, even as he laid plans to revolutionize French society as the leader of the Socialist Party, thus lent legitimacy to the charge of cowardice or passivity on the part of state Jews concerned to preserve their social status. Apparently echoing this extremely negative judgment, Julien Benda had this to say one year later:

> The eagerness of Jews back then to show "who they were"—to flock to government schools and the Council of State—was one of the chief causes of their future misfortunes, symbolized most powerfully by the Dreyfus Affair. The Reinachs' triumph in the *concours général* [school entrance examination] strikes me as one of the essential sources of the anti-Semitism that would erupt fifteen years later.[30]

Hannah Arendt also wrote about the alleged pusillanimity of French Jews during the Dreyfus Affair. But Blum was more familiar than Arendt with the distinctive nature of the French state, so it is more surprising that he, like her, attacked the character of the state Jews to whose ranks he himself belonged. He strangely ignored the steadfastness of many of his colleagues in the civilian and military bureaucracy, who openly protested against anti-Semitic activities, signing petitions, fighting with their fists, and even challenging their adversaries to duels with pistol and sword. André Spire, for instance, Blum's colleague on the Council of State, fought a duel after the nationalist, anti-Semitic newspaper *La Libre Parole* published an article on "Jews Before the Council of State."[31] Far from burying their heads in the sand, many of them—including academics, members of the civil service elite, and high-ranking military officers—openly flouted the requirement that government servants refrain from commenting on political matters and joined not only in the defense of Dreyfus but even more importantly in the condemnation of anti-Semitism. As late as 1935, Blum was apparently still unaware of the Committee of Defense against Anti-Semitism, which had been created in December 1894 with the explicit accord of Grand Rabbi Zadoc Kahn and led by the former prefect Isaïe Levaillant.[32] Other Jewish officials joined the fight on behalf of Dreyfus through the Ligue des Droits de l'Homme et du Citoyen (Human Rights League), of which Blum was himself a founding member and to which he remained faithful for twenty-six years.[33]

To be sure, everyone in France was preoccupied with the consequences of World War I, the Great Depression, and the rise of fascism: the extreme right was back, French political parties were in disarray, and threats were looming on all sides. Between the abortive right-wing coup attempt of February 6, 1934, and the victory of the Popular Front in the spring of 1936, Léon Blum, the uncontested leader of the socialist movement, was thus plunged back into the passionate turbulence of his youth, echoes of which haunted him in the present. Others who had played leading roles in the Dreyfus Affair had the same feeling. On July 14, 1935, in the same month that Blum began recounting his "Memories of the Affair," the Rassemblement Populaire (People's Coalition) was born: left-wing parties and unions joined forces in defense of freedom. Victor Basch, the president of the Human Rights League, which had been created in 1898 to counter the threat of the Ligue de la Patrie Française (League of the French Fatherland), spoke to demonstrators on the day after Dreyfus's death: "What is important is that Dreyfusism lives on. . . . I have seen nothing since the Affair to rival its importance." In that same month Basch also wrote that "today, we are in a situation analogous to that of the Affair. Once again, the enemies of the democratic republic are on the march. The names are different but the men are the same, the parties are the same, the hatreds are the same, the appetites are the same. The fascists of today are the Boulangists and anti-Dreyfusards of yesterday."[34]

Here we see clearly how tenacious the memory of the Dreyfus Affair remained. Blum repeatedly made the same comparison. In his book, he alluded several times to the affair's relevance to the world "today." In the aftermath of the abortive coup of February 6, 1934, he remarked that the anti-Semitic movement once led by Drumont "continues today in Hitlerian racism," which he saw as a strong influence on the heirs of the anti-Dreyfusards.[35] In the eyes of many, history seemed to be repeating itself, but this time the threat was even more radical —so radical as to give rise to moments of collective psychosis in France.

3

———◆◆◆———

On Love

BEFORE BLUM became the historical figure we know, he was a student of amorous passion, ardently dedicated to his research. For him, the Dreyfus Affair was over. Having passed the entrance exam for the Council of State in December 1895 and joined the civil service, he was able to devote much of his time to literary criticism, writing numerous book reviews and indulging his passion for the theater. He collected his reviews in two books, *En lisant* (While Reading) and *Au théâtre* (At the Theater), and wrote several short stories. He was barely twenty in September 1892 when he published his first long essay in the *Revue Blanche*. The subject was the relation of dream to action in the quest for happiness—a quest that "gave [Stendhal's heroes] Fabrice del Dongo and Julien Sorel their passionate inner drive."[1] In the same vein, a short while later, he published a story titled "Ceci et cela" (This and That), which recounted the amorous uncertainties of a confused young man "in the habit of looking to *The Red and the Black* for advice on how to behave. . . . Every evening, Julien Sorel aroused in me an intoxicating taste [for passion]. Little by little, my own life became confused with his. His was the voice of reason inside my head." The young hero therefore decides to do as Julien did and take the hand of his own Madame de Rênal before the clock strikes ten, because otherwise "Julien would be ashamed of me."[2] Young Blum, just embarking on a literary career, identified body and soul with Stendhal's hero. He also began work on a book about Stendhal.

The author of *The Red and the Black*, *Lucien Leuwen*, and *The Charterhouse of Parma* appealed to Blum, just as he appealed to Proust. The relationship between Proust and Blum—two young Jews of roughly the same age who shared the same passion for Stendhal and who sometimes wrote about quite similar subjects—had its ups and downs.[3] Following the example of Stendhal's *De l'amour* (On Love), Proust included a long section "Sur l'amour" (On Love) in *Jean Santeuil*, a preliminary study for his *Search*, while Blum at about the same time published *Du mariage* (On Marriage), which caused a scandal in 1907. Both Proust and Blum saw Stendhal as a professor of energy, a champion of youth, individualism, and passion. The theorist of egotism influenced Jean, the hero of *Jean Santeuil*, who "thought of him constantly" while courting Mme S, taking greater pleasure "from his love than his lover"—pleasure whose "intensity he had discovered in Julien Sorel, Fabrice Del Dongo, and *De l'amour*."[4]

Blum's admiration for Stendhal was more constant than Proust's, however. Unlike Proust, Blum admired the willfulness of Stendhal's characters, whose desires were not limited to the imagination. In 1914, years after publishing his Stendhalian short stories, Blum published a tribute to Stendhal, *Stendhal et le beylisme* (Stendhal and Beylism). In that same year Proust published the first volume of his *Search*, in which he parted company with Stendhal by granting the imagination priority over action.[5] Blum thus diverged not only from Proust but also from Barrès, even more than he had done in 1898—Barrès who had been his first "teacher," his "elder brother," an erstwhile Stendhalian who had readily abandoned the "cult of the self" for that of the nation and who had become an adept of biological determinism and a critic of "the uprooted." Blum invoked the example of Julien Sorel to argue that "uprooting" à la Stendhal could be a source of energy.[6] Blum saw himself reflected entirely in Stendhal, who took the place of Barrès as the "admired brother": "We loved him," he wrote. "His influence became part of our life and in a strange way we perhaps infused his work with a charm that existed only in ourselves, in our youth and our talent."[7]

This substitution of one "brother" for another marked a decisive moment in Blum's life: having broken with Barrès, who had become a nationalist, Blum henceforth resolved to place his passion and energy at the service of love—love not only of woman but also of social justice, which Barrès, having joined the radical anti-Semitic right, turned his back on. According to a leading Stendhal specialist, Léon Blum, the future leader of the French nation, became "the first true Stendhalian of modern times."[8] Another wrote: "The dream that comes true in maturity, the potential of youth kept miraculously intact, the tension between the demands of logic, necessary for action, and the tenderness of the heart that blunts the virtues of reason—these traits of Stendhal's character Léon Blum recognized as his own."[9]

Blum revealed his fondness for the author of *The Red and the Black* in countless ways.[10] Like the young Stendhal, "he had the look and vulnerability of a girl of fourteen" coupled with "a chaotic emotional life." Like Stendhal, "he had the delicate nerves and sensitive skin of a woman. He acquired and never lost the habit of daydreaming, a taste for the inner life, or rather for dialogue with himself, and an attitude toward life at once greedy and passive, born of a vague expectation of happiness."[11] As Blum saw it, Stendhal "developed an extreme sensitivity," like Blum himself, thus fostering his *espagnolisme*—the proud, combative, easily offended yet generous character exemplified by El Cid. Stendhal, Blum insists, was "a man of tranquil, quiet courage . . . his sensitivity and physical susceptibility were extreme."[12] Blum shared this "tranquil courage."[13] Like Stendhal's heroes, he refused to be mocked and avenged insults at the point of a sword. It is hardly surprising that Julien Sorel, Fabrice del Dongo, and above all Lucien Leuwen haunted his imagination, since all three engaged in multiple duels. Like Stendhal himself and his hero Lucien Leuwen, Blum despised the *juste milieu* (middle-of-the-roaders) and the social hierarchies that crushed individual talent, ambition, and passion. Like Stendhal, he denounced the contemptuous attitudes of the powerful toward the people and the way they induced young people to compromise their passions.

Blum also shared Stendhal's contempt for money and commerce and Fabrice and Lucien's cult of the French Revolution, which challenged the social order and set young men free to pursue their destinies. Stendhal dreamed of another revolution, while Blum would enjoy the privilege of leading one: the Popular Front, which he inspired, struck a significant blow at the power of the ruling class and marked a giant step forward for the happiness of the individual and the society.[14] It was in a sense the realization of the Saint-Simonian project of which Lucien Leuwen dreamed. And also like Stendhal, Blum at the end of his life would pride himself on never having owned anything or accumulated any wealth—apart from his books.[15]

Stendhal and Blum thus shared many traits. Stendhal quickly abandoned his plan to enter the École Polytechnique. Blum behaved in such a way that he was expelled from the École Normale Supérieure in his first year. The proctor's reports make reference to numerous absences: "did not return," "absent," "Blum late." "Little Bob" preferred the ballroom to the study and found himself repeatedly "confined" to his room before finally being expelled.[16] Yet Blum, like Stendhal, became one of the Council of State's respected auditors. Both were government lawyers noted for their rigorous legal analyses, yet neither renounced the object of his passion, the desperate search for happiness, or "the avid need for love fostered by reading and fed by daydreaming, a product of the imagination alone."[17] Love was thus the greatest thing in both men's lives—love anticipated, sought after, and conquered in open combat. Stendhal the romantic nevertheless failed to win the women he loved: his mistresses slipped through his fingers, and love remained for him more a figment of the imagination than a fixture of his life. Blum, though he failed to respect the stages of "crystallization" prescribed by his "brother" Stendhal, was nevertheless successful in love. As he saw it, Stendhal "never experienced the overwhelming power of the senses, which the woman senses in a confused way and which drives the man to take risks."[18]

Throughout his life, Blum was seen as decisive and enterprising, yet he always remained the daydreaming adolescent he once was, embodying the boldness of Julien Sorel, the courage of Fabrice del Dongo, and the dreams of Lucien Leuwen. More than Stendhal, who recoiled from action, he embodied these Stendhalian heroes' youth, dreams of happiness, and optimism, which became the rule he lived by even in his most tragic moments. In the end, while Proust believed that Stendhal's writing accorded too much importance to action and to the object of love while ignoring its purely imaginative basis, Blum fraternally reproached Stendhal for his lack of audacity. This difference sealed the fate of these two young Jews, who crossed paths on a number of occasions toward the end of the nineteenth century: Proust locked himself in his apartment and wrote the many volumes of the *Search*, a vast imaginative fresco in which homosexual passion and Jewish identity were intertwined, while Blum left the literary world for that of "imperious" amorous conquest and political power.[19] One withdrew into the privacy of his apartment, in which he chose to confine himself, while the other resolutely chose the course of action in the public sphere.

An ardent young man, Léon Blum threw himself into the quest for love, about which he wrote many short stories, most of which remained unpublished. In one of them, a student at the École Normale Supérieure courts a woman named Marie-Thérèse. "As her mouth fastened itself to mine, she said, 'I love you, I love you too much.'" In a fit of jealousy, the student leaves his lover without a word of farewell. Blum's love stories were fiction possibly tinged with reality. He imagined other loves: Denise, Laure, Francine, Eliane. In writing *Du mariage* (On Marriage, 1907), his paean to love, desire, physical pleasure, and liberation of the instincts, he took his inspiration not only from Fabrice and Julien but also from Don Juan and Valmont in *Liaisons dangereuses* (Dangerous Liaisons) and Tolstoy's *Anna Karenina*.[20] Blum courageously assailed arranged marriages and matches based on financial interests, bourgeois conventions that oppressed women by forcing them to remain virgins until they married. He was sharply critical of taboos that impinged on the sexual freedom of women. He did not denounce the institution of marriage but insisted that happiness and compatibility between husband and wife could be achieved only if both were permitted to "sow their wild oats" and learn the ways of sexuality before giving up their freedom and committing themselves to marriage. Otherwise, marriage would remain an inegalitarian institution subject to all kinds of betrayal, with adultery as a substitute for youthful experience forbidden by conventions that compelled young men to frequent prostitutes—a radical antithesis of satisfying amorous passion. As Blum saw it, for both men and women "a life of adventure should precede married life; a life of instinct should precede a life of reason."[21] The transition from natural polygamy to institutionalized monogamy therefore concerned both sexes. A thoroughgoing feminist *avant la lettre* contrary to most of his socialist fellows, as well as an adept of Fourier's theories of love, Blum vilified the hypocrisy of the bourgeoisie and insisted that the sexual liberation of women was the only way to change male sexuality and ensure the happiness of both partners in marriage. Although he took his inspiration from Balzac's celebrated *La physiologie du mariage* (The Physiology of Marriage), he often relied on his "brother" Stendhal for descriptions of the meandering ways of passion.

"I loved to follow women," Blum wrote in *On Marriage*, "because I was a sentimental dreamer ever hopeful that a chance encounter at a street corner might lead to an adventure that would alter the course of my life."[22] Emulating Julien Sorel, he recounted—or invented—an amorous adventure of his own. On spotting in the street a woman dressed in black whom he found to his taste, in this account, he decided to follow her. After several hours the beautiful stranger turns, strikes up a conversation, and informs the young man that she has two hours to spare before boarding a train to join her husband in the provinces. The two then calmly repair to a hotel near the station—a hotel chosen by the woman, who had often stayed there with her husband. There they become lovers. The man then tells this story to one of his friends, who immediately guesses his secret: the beautiful stranger can only be the young wife of a common friend of theirs from law school, who has recently been named to a post as judge in a small provincial town. Despite the letters he receives from his mistress, the man decides to break off the affair, which has revealed the unfortunate consequence of a bad marriage: the woman, indifferent to her husband's caresses, is utterly lacking in sensuality. "This story is true," Blum continued. "I had profited . . . from what was probably a fairly common case of physical disharmony brought on by the first experience of marriage. . . . I try to imagine the inept gravity and expeditiously ceremonious clumsiness with which [my friend] must have treated the little girl who had stumbled into his marriage bed."[23]

In another story Blum told in *On Marriage* of his abortive encounter with the beautiful Colette, who, unlike Julien Sorel, did not "dare": "You should have dared, Colette. As a worthy and experienced lover . . . I deserved to taste the fruits that you, in spite of your own heart's desire, felt you had to reserve for another man. With what irresistible voluptuous sweetness you would have bestowed on me the nuptial gift of yourself! Your husband would have come into your life later, as he did. You would have been able to contemplate marriage without terror."[24] Blum did not hesitate to conclude with a triumphant, if not very feminist, flourish: "By imposing the severest of penalties on women, you prevent them from gaining knowledge of the ways of love before they marry, but in so doing you spoil their image of their future master."[25]

To anti-Semites, Blum's book was an attack on the family intended to justify the seduction of young French women by Jews. *La Croix des Alpes-Maritimes* wrote that, despite Alfred Naquet (who was instrumental in legalizing divorce in France) and Alfred Dreyfus,

> certain traditions of honor and virtue remain in the French soul and can be rooted out only by dint of great effort. This is to be the work of Israel's thinkers. . . . One of these fugitives from the ghetto, Léon Blum, has written a shocking book. . . . The Jew can be content with his work. Working within nations that welcome him, unconscious of the danger he represents, this foreign guest, who shares neither their blood nor their race and can never assimilate . . . goes about his deadly business.

According to *La Libre Parole*, "with this contribution to the new, secular, not to say Hebraic morality, M. Blum has just been decorated by M. Briand." *Le Peuple Français* proclaimed that Blum's book had brought "pornography into the Council of State." A writer for *Jaune* took a derisive tone: "I, for one, readily accept the theory if its application is limited to young kikes of both sexes. . . . Why shouldn't Blum go joyfully to the Victoire synagogue after Sabbath services with slides in hand to teach his lessons to the offspring of the Israélite 'aristocracy' and high finance."[26] Léon Daudet wrote that the book was the work "of an immoralist entirely alien to our mores, customs, and usages, indeed to common sense as it is understood in the West."[27] Blum was dismissed as an "Asiatic" with oriental habits and un-Christian harems. Even his friend André Gide felt that the work proved that "the Jews are past masters of the art of dismantling our most respected and venerable institutions, the institutions on which our western civilization rests."[28] *Du mariage* provoked a reaction of disgust: it could only have been written by a Turk or a Persian.[29] Blum the Parisian dandy and socialite who spent his evenings in the most fashionable salons was thus transformed into his opposite: an alien from the East. The languid ephebe mocked by many of his contemporaries was revealed as a dangerous "Don Juan of the synagogue."[30] Moderate national newspapers such as *Le Figaro* and *Le Temps* treated the book more favorably, acknowledging that it did not question the institution of marriage but merely suggested that marriage should take place only after a preliminary stage of amorous relations in which the future husband and wife would become "sincere friends . . . and loyal partners."[31]

Combining savory and tragic tales with philosophical ruminations, *Du mariage* was nothing less than a call for the sexual liberation of women and for equality of the sexes in love, which Blum claimed was the only way to prevent divorce. He saw himself as serving the cause of justice by defending the innocence of women unfairly treated, as Dreyfus had been, by ruling class norms. From there he would go on to broaden his quest for justice to society as a whole: his socialist politics can thus be seen as an extension of his engagement in the Dreyfus Affair and in the cause of women's liberation. A lover of justice in general, Blum was first a lover of women. We know little about Blum as Don Juan. We do know, as he himself admitted, that he "liked to follow women." In the Paris police archives, which contain many reports of slanderous rumors, one finds allegations that he later kept a mistress and engaged in perverse activities with another woman.[32] Such fragmentary and deeply biased reports are open to doubt and afford little or no glimpse of what Blum's love life was actually like. But the question remains: How closely did Blum follow his own precepts in regard to marriage?

He married three times, in three distinct phases of his life. Each of his wives was Jewish, but their temperaments differed sharply.[33] Made rather jealous by the early marriage of his friend Gide, Blum married Lise Bloch in February 1896, when he was a young man of twenty-four with limited experience.[34] Neglecting his own principles, he married a girl from the Jewish bourgeoisie who had scarcely had time to "sow her wild oats." He had known her since childhood. She recalled meeting him for the first time at a holiday celebration in Marly-le-Roi when she was in the ninth grade: "Léon had soft, cloudy eyes. He was already near-sighted but unaware of it and did not wear glasses. His mouth was indistinct, his lips slightly parted, his voice caressing and self-assured, combining childish appeal with a note of manly insolence. He was already prodigiously intelligent and witty, with truly unbelievable ease and authority."[35]

Lise belonged to a well-to-do Jewish family of Alsatian origin, several of whose members held high government posts. The wedding at the Paris Synagogue on the Rue de la Victoire was an impressive affair, celebrated by the Grand Rabbi of Paris, as was customary among this class of Jews ("les fous de la République").[36] Léon received a substantial sum of money from his parents as a wedding gift, while Lise brought a large dowry into the marriage and stood to inherit a good deal more. After a delightful honeymoon in Italy, the young couple were thus able to move into a comfortable apartment on what is today the Rue Guynemer opposite the Luxembourg Gardens before moving into an even better apartment on the Boulevard du Montparnasse. They went out often and enjoyed many cultural and social events together, largely in the company of other Jews. Music was a regular feature of their life: Maurice Ravel, Gabriel Fauré, Alfred Cortot, and Reynaldo Hahn were frequent visitors, as were colleagues (many of them Jewish) from the *Revue Blanche* and the Council of State. Together with friends they went to the theater, staged plays at home, danced, sang, gave parties in a rented villa near Chartres, and enjoyed vacations.[37] Blum, apparently at Lise's behest, backed away from his commitment to socialism in order to devote himself to literary criticism and his work for the Council of State.

The marriage seemed to be going well, indeed so well that Blum dedicated *Du mariage* to his wife, describing himself as a "happy" and "grateful man." Lise impressed others as a brilliant, elegant, fragile, and cultivated woman. In 1902 the couple had a son, Robert, whom they did not circumcise and to whom Blum would remain close throughout his life. He eventually attended the École Polytechnique and became a brilliant engineer.

Nevertheless, what had seemed an idyllic marriage exempt from the pitfalls and disappointments Blum analyzed in his book ultimately collapsed. In notes he made while preparing to write *Du mariage*, we find this pregnant sequence: "Lise last night. The moment there is suffering, there is anger and a desire for vengeance. But no. Nastiness is no nobler when one is suffering than when one is not."[38] It was apparently during the summer of 1911, if not earlier, that Blum began a passionate relationship with Thérèse Pereyra, which lasted until Lise, whose health had long been precarious, died in 1931. Thérèse, whose sister married the composer Paul Dukas, came from a wealthy Sephardic family and was one of the Blums' closest friends. They had known each other for years, sang together, and vacationed in the same places. She had always been in love with Léon but out of spite married Edmond Mayrargues when she was twenty-six (she, too, had not "sown her wild oats").

Blum embarked on a double life filled with the kinds of lies and compromises of bourgeois marriage he mocked in his book.[39] Thérèse was as different as can be from Lise: indifferent to literature, she was a militant socialist who would transform Blum's life. She encouraged him to commit himself more deeply to politics and to give up his literary criticism and socializing.[40] As in a bad drawing-room comedy, Lise apparently stumbled on Léon's secret in 1914 when she chanced to find a letter from Thérèse: after a violent scene of jealousy, Léon embarked on a banal and typically bourgeois double life, which continued for many years.[41] Constance Coline, the daughter of a friend of the Blums, tells a story that might have been taken from the stage. In her words, "Léon allowed the storm to pass, was kind and understanding toward Lise, but resolved" not to break with Thérèse while at the same time remaining married to Lise. Waspishly, Coline added that "Lise hung on for dear life, thereby poisoning the lives of the other two."[42]

The correspondence, much of it unpublished, between Blum and his wife on one hand and Blum and his mistress on the other reveals a great deal about the double life of the author of *Du mariage*. For more than twenty years—a crucial period in Blum's life, during which he became a deputy, succeeded Jean Jaurès as leader of the Socialist Party, dealt with the aftermath of the schism in the Socialist International following the Bol-

shevik victory in Russia, and began his march toward power—
Blum exchanged with both Lise and Thérèse letters filled with
amorous passion as well as despair and resignation. Unfortunately, not all of these letters are dated, although the postmarks
are legible on some. Sometimes the content of a letter allows us
to deduce approximately when it was sent.

During the war years, Thérèse's passion knew no bounds.
She eagerly awaited his return whenever he left her to spend
time with his family: "My love, my love. I've just heard the
sound of your voice. It's Léon. I jumped for joy. How I jumped!
It was on the phone! How cruel it is to be so close and yet so
far. . . . I desperately reach out to you. How long until this
Christmas vacation is over?"[43] In another letter she wrote: "My
thoughts are with you at every moment. They are quite sad, I
assure you. But you love me, I know. . . . I am reading [your
book on] Stendhal. . . . I admire every sentence. Everything
you've written there is extraordinary."[44] From the military hos-
pital where she began volunteering as a nurse in September
1914, she wrote among the dead and wounded: "Sir, I love you.
That is what I wanted to say. I could say the same thing in
every line of this letter. I could shout it to everyone I see."[45] In
another letter she wrote: "There, Sir, is your destiny. You are
condemned to be loved by this little slip of a woman whether
you like it or not. But you like it, don't you, my heart?"[46] When
her work allowed, she wrote: "The state I'm in when you're
pressed against me. Darling, darling, I realize that I love you
more every day. I am yours."[47]

She suffered from Léon's double life and even from the
time he devoted to his family: "When will these separations
end? . . . When will we live together in the country? I have
thought about living in a house as simple as this one, even in
a landscape like this one, with trees swaying in the wind along
the river and the monotony of country roads and fields. . . . You
would be very happy, I know, and so would I. But let's not speak

of it."[48] She did speak of it constantly though, even if it meant having to apologize to her lover: "I am also furious with myself for bringing this issue up again. You are probably saying that I must be furious a lot. It's true. But it's so hard to give it up."[49] Her unconditional love rebelled: "I find I love you more and more every day, I'm filled with love for you, steeped in it, intoxicated by it. When will I see you, my darling?"[50] Signs of her dissatisfaction are constant: "If only you would reassure me, if only you would console me. Your words and caresses make me forget everything else. . . . As you can see, the days pass, and I endure every kind of anguish."[51] Her complaints are never ending. Worried that Blum will not be returning the next day because he has been detained in Bordeaux, where the government had relocated during the war, she wrote: "Oh, darling, do not make me suffer this way. Be here tomorrow. I am yours."[52]

The double life continued, but Blum in love protected his family. Thérèse could do nothing to stop him, and she suffered for it: "I know that when you return, I will not have you, I will not see you, and I will be jealous—jealous and unhappy. But I love you."[53]

The same carton in the archives contains many letters from Blum to his wife Lise with descriptions of meetings and of days spent in provincial hotels: "An old-fashioned hotel on a small provincial square with a fine old Gothic church of red stone. The furniture and look of the place are provincial, but the comfort is real, the bed good, the room nice and warm, and in the morning there is fresh butter with good rolls."[54] Blum worried about Lise's comfort on vacation: "What I do not want at all is for any concern with economy to compromise the comfort of your stay. On this point I feel I must use my power as head of the family to issue an order." In the same letter he added: "Tell our son that his letter is very amusing and very nice and gave me a great deal of pleasure. . . . I still insist on extreme caution in regard to sports, walks, and physical exertion of any sort."[55] Although Blum occasionally alluded to his "somewhat troubling state of uncertainty," he more often than not discussed the weather: "A storm is raging here. A classic storm, or, rather, a romantic one: sheets of rain, wild wind, tempestuous seas."[56] He also wrote frequently about his travels in the provinces, Lise's colds and other health problems, walks in the country, fatigue, relaxation, and sleep. And he sometimes offered words of advice: "Tell our son . . . not to eat too much candy."[57] He also offered to teach his son how to box.[58] There is little or nothing about his political activities or his polemics, and still less about his private life. In one letter written in 1917, he reported on an evening spent in society: "At Hayn's I ran into a charming Lucien Daudet, whom I had not seen for 25 years, with whom I was able to speak quite freely about his brother. Marcel Proust was expected but did not come. . . . It was a charming evening, filled with conversations of the sort we used to have. Hayn sang for two hours."[59] And many of the letters are quite banal, like this one sent on September 31, 1916: "I hope the journey did not make your cold worse and that you did not suffer from the chill. Here it snowed tonight. The cliffs were all white this morning down to the sea, but it is not cold outside now."[60]

Blum wanted to preserve his marriage no matter what. The idea of divorce never crossed his mind. He remained deeply attached to Lise and his son Robert even though he was passionately in love with Thérèse. Throughout the affair he kept Thérèse apprised of what was happening. On August 24, 1920, he wrote: "Lise is in a bad way. Nervous fever with anxiety and depression. I hardly leave her side, which is why you've had so little news from me. My love, I think of you with all my might . . . as when we last parted. I love you, sweetheart."[61] A few days later he wrote: "Lise is in a very bad way. Anxiety, nerves, almost invincible insomnia. . . . I was able to go out this morning for a short walk, so I stopped at the post office to dash off this note. I am yours, sweetheart."[62] The story came close to vaudeville: forgotten were the theories of Fourier and the paeans to happy monogamous marriage.

Blum suspected that Lise could no longer put up with his betrayals. On June 23, 1921, he wrote: "What I want to say is how astonished and dumbfounded I was not to find you at home Tuesday evening. I expected nothing of the kind. I had no inkling when I arrived. I turned the key in the lock. I was surprised to find the house so dark. Robert came to investigate the noise. I asked him how you were. He told me you had taken the 8 PM train. I could hardly breathe. . . . Can you believe that it was not until I woke up this morning that I saw the note pinned to my pillow. All those months, even after our worst days, I, too, slept comfortably and happily by your side. Good bye. Until soon, as Porto says. I kiss you, little one."[63] As appointment after appointment is broken, the tension is palpable: "Darling, we are obliged to have lunch with Jaurès and others. There's no way to get out of it."[64] These repeated and often unexplained absences irritated Lise. Blum tried to justify himself: "My little Lise, Last night I received your letter of Wednesday morning and this morning your letter of Wednesday night. Both hurt my feelings. You seem to doubt that I really wanted to be with you. . . . The only thing that kept me away was the extreme fatigue I experienced after the poisoning I endured Sunday night. . . . I hug you tightly, little Lise, and I, too, feel like crying."[65] Lise was not taken in: "I received your letter of yesterday, which told me nothing about your reasons for not coming on Sunday for a three-day stay, as I so ardently desired. You don't seem at all upset that the dates of your treatment have been changed."[66] Loneliness oppressed her: "Coming home to a big, empty house . . . I am not used to coming home alone, little Léon."[67]

In 1923, she went off to Italy by herself but could not stand her life of misery: "My life is slipping away, and I'm far from you, and I'm afraid to be close. Your little Lise is indebted to you for much happiness, but if you only knew how she suffers."[68] In October of the same year, her pain, which stemmed in part from her illness, became unbearable: "Help me to preserve the dignity and beauty of our life, which privately as well as socially must be protected from this illness, however long it lasts."[69] Abandoned, Lise sank into depression. Her handwriting became almost illegible: "My little Léon, I have done a great deal of thinking this past week. I do not want to be a burden on you. That would be unfair and wrong. No one has the right to use suffering as a weapon ready to be unleashed at any moment." And this: "My friend Léon, I entrust our life to you. Do what is best. I will accept your choice and will do everything in my power to accept it without anger, rancor, or sadness."[70] And then on July 30, 1925, came this sublime letter, marking the culmination of their de facto separation:

> You ask me how I am doing. I live in almost constant worry and anxiety about what my life will become. I have decided to give up the fight. I am so exhausted by the continuation and repetition of the same injuries and the same wounds that I no longer have the courage to endure.
>
> When I left you, I told you as tenderly and forthrightly as I could how much I love you and how hard I tried during these five awful years. You seemed to understand me. Your horrible response in regard to the question of vacations was even more painful to me than the other times, and the way you arranged the vacation violated the wretched pact we've made every two years amid much emotion and many protestations of our desire to remain together.
>
> Little Léon, I cannot stay with you any longer. I left in December because I was in too much pain. I asked you to leave in May because I was in too much pain. . . .
>
> I am afraid that my feeling for you, which filled my former life, will eventually perish and I will be deprived not

only of a present reality but also of the sweet memories that sustain my existence.

What will you say to me tomorrow that will hurt me even more?

And then, you see, impinging on your freedom, your taste, and your thoughts, spying on you, stealing moments you would rather spend elsewhere—all this is unworthy of us and not what I want for myself.

Since I am no longer your comfort or your "reality," as you said on rue d'Assas, nor your pleasure, it's better that I go away. Do not take this as an ultimatum or a sign of bitterness or even a reproach. See it as the utterance of a spent force, a tottering human being, a disappointed hope with no longer enough life left in it to be revived once more.

Farewell, my child. My faithful old heart calls out to you and clasps you to it one more time.

Your true wife.[71]

Despite this, they continued to present themselves as a couple to the outside world and stumble through various social obligations.

Meanwhile, though, Blum had launched his drive for power. Campaigning in Narbonne in March and April of 1929, he gave speech after speech, traveled long distances, and took part in countless rallies, but through it all he never stopped writing to Thérèse: "I think only of you, my beloved."[72] He harangued crowds while hecklers tried to prevent him from speaking: "Such are my nights in Narbonne," he wrote Thérèse. "If all goes well on Sunday, only three or four more days to go. My God, how slowly things go. How I need to hold you close."[73] A month later, on April 15, 1929, he wrote: "I think only of seeing you again, my beloved. I love you."[74] Blum was obsessed with Thérèse. In the heat of the campaign his only fear was that he would be unable to join her: "I hate this business, which will deprive me tomorrow of what I was so ardently anticipating and will also bitterly disappoint you."[75] On March 5, 1929, he wrote from Marseille: "The welcome I am receiving everywhere is moving. Impossible not to be warmed by it. . . . I am either working like a machine or thinking of you, my beloved. I adore you."[76]

Tired from campaigning and mingling with people, he finally managed to get away for a rendezvous with Thérèse in Toulouse, where he reserved two rooms at the Hôtel Terminus: "If you only knew how stubborn and clever I had to be to steal these two days from the pitiless Montel and all the idiots here who dog my every step and want to exhibit me everywhere and go wherever I go."[77] (Eugène Montel later succeeded Blum as deputy from the district.) At the same time he described his political tour from Toulon to Marseille to Lise in rather different terms, saying that he traveled "over atrocious roads through an atrocious mistral . . . breaking down yet again in the most deserted place in the world."[78] His wife's silence worried him: "You tell me that Robert is charming. I know it. What I want to know is how *you* are doing and feeling. I think you were deliberately silent about this, and I don't really know why. Anyway, until tomorrow. I hug you, my dear, closely and affectionately."[79]

Lise was ill, however, and declining rapidly despite treatment. She died in December 1931. From France and abroad Blum received a vast number of condolences for his loss.[80]

Thérèse followed the daily progress of Léon's campaign and commented as a committed militant on the traps that were being laid for him. From a distance she railed against his rivals: "You tell me that you don't feel these attacks. . . . But since you've put in so much effort, it would be good if you were successful. Once again, all the bastards are joining forces against you."[81] A few days later, she returned to the same subject: "Naturally, they've formed a coalition against you. I expected it. I'm anxious for you. What bastards, what hypocrites."[82] She feared for Blum's health and deplored the fact that his district was so far from Paris: "I admit that I'm anxious that you are on the road so much. . . . Tell your driver to be careful, I implore you. I know that you are reckless."[83] When Blum held many rallies in Bordeaux, she wrote: "You are overworked. . . . Leave some of the dirty work to the novices who revolve around you without doing anything. I don't want them to overwork my lover. I am capable of the worst if anything should happen to you."[84] Passionate about politics and deeply involved in its day-to-day struggles, she advised Blum and freely criticized his enemies— the "bastards" who attacked him.[85]

In December 1932, a year after Lise's death, Thérèse became "citizen Thérèse Léon Blum," and from then on she appeared with Blum at all his Popular Front rallies and in official photographs. She answered letters from his district, handled his correspondence, and intervened with government agencies on behalf of constituents. She played a growing political role, which took on even greater importance when he came to power in 1936, at which point her role became public. The couple settled into a life of militant politics and loving companionship.[86] It was a time of radical change in France, which saw marked improvement in the lower classes' standard of living. People sang and danced despite the threats from abroad. The relationship between Léon and Thérèse was one of perfect understanding. Their worldviews were identical and their love was complete. But Thérèse, too, fell ill and, fatigued and extenuated by her punishing schedule, died of a heart attack on January 22, 1938, leaving Blum lonely and dejected.

Having "followed women" in his youth and having been an insatiable lover all his life, Blum that same year resumed his connection with Jeanne Levylier, who in their younger years had moved in the same Jewish circles as Léon and Lise Blum. Twice divorced and highly intelligent, Jeanne became the socialist leader's girlfriend. She would remain with him until the end of his life, through still more tragic ordeals. "Janot," as she was called, was more discreet than Thérèse and similar in many ways to Lise. She was a woman of exemplary courage and unswerving loyalty in most difficult times. Janot supported Blum during his imprisonment at Chazeron under the Vichy regime. She followed him to the Château du Portalet, where she visited him every day, and joined him at Buchenwald, where she took good care of him.[87] In that sinister setting, they were granted special authorization to marry on October 5, 1943. As Germany's military position worsened, Janot remained with Léon despite the risks. Liberated at last by American troops after a dramatic evacuation to Dachau, they returned to France together on May 14, 1945, and resumed their quiet life together, a far cry from the passions of earlier times.

4

The Heir of Jaurès: The Socialist Commitment

THE WOMAN Léon Blum remained closest to was perhaps his mother, a woman imbued with a deep sense of ethics and a profound respect for justice. Late in life, he told an anecdote from his childhood in which an apple symbolizes the values his mother transmitted to him and his brother.

> My mother also had a profound influence on me. She was the most just person I have ever known. . . . My mother's sense of justice was acute: when she gave my brother and me two apples to share, she would cut each apple in two and give each of us half of each apple. Since reaching the age of reason I have always dreamed of someday giving every person in France the two half-apples to which he or she is entitled. Call those apples Order and Liberty: that was the socialism I learned as a child. Being raised by such a mother, I acquired a sense of justice very early in life.[1]

The socialism Blum learned as a child from a mother attached to a messianic tradition of human redemption awakened his conscience and led him to join the Dreyfusard cause. On April 11, 1899, at the height of the Dreyfus Affair, which had made such a mockery of justice, Blum reflected on the role Jews had played in the battle to prove the captain's innocence.

> To enlightened people, [religion] means nothing anymore. Yet the race is deeply believing, eminently capable of faith. . . . [This faith] is entirely rational. It can be summed up in a word: Justice. The Jew's religion is Justice. . . . His Messiah is nothing other than a symbol of Eternal Justice. . . . It is this world, the living world of the present with its old people and old trees that must one day establish an order based on Reason, that must subject everyone to the same rules and give each person his or her due. Isn't that the spirit of socialism? It is the ancient spirit of the race. . . . It was not a lapse on the part of Providence that Marx and Lassalle were Jews.[2]

Although Blum himself had grown estranged from the dogma and ritual of Judaism, he clearly insisted in this youthful text that Judaism, justice, and socialism were related. As he put it, "the race that gave birth to Judith, having confined our existence to life here below, wishes to see justice established on this earth."[3] In unpublished lectures he refers to "the prophetic tradition of the Jews."[4] His encounters first with Lucien Herr and later with Jean Jaurès came as revelations that confirmed his maternal heritage. Both were socialists as well as ardent Dreyfusards. Herr, the librarian of the École Normale Supérieure, played a crucial role, encouraging an entire generation of young *normaliens* to join the socialist movement. In October 1897, he introduced Blum to Jaurès, who was thirty-eight at the time. Both had attended the École. As Blum later recalled, "I was twenty-five. At the time I had a precious gift, the gift of admiration. I admired Jaurès with all my might. I desperately wanted to know him. We quickly became friends, but friendship on my side always remained tinged with an indelible element of respect."[5] Jaurès and Blum saw each other constantly in the small circle of permanently active Dreyfusards. They visited each other's homes and often had lunch together. It was Blum's influence that brought Jaurès into the Dreyfusard circle, which resembled a Parisian salon and was therefore utterly different from the provincial peasant and working-class society that Jaurès represented. Despite some initial hesitation, Jaurès ultimately became one of the most ardent members of the group. In *Preuves* (Proofs), he demolished the prosecution's case and changed the trajectory of the affair forever.

If the goal of assimilated Jews was justice, as Blum claimed, the vehicle that many chose to achieve it was the humanistic socialism embodied by Jaurès. Few were Marxists, in part because Marxism attached little importance to republican universalism and in part because it failed to give national identity its due. Jewish socialists identified with Jaurèsian messianism, a direct descendant of the French Revolution they so greatly admired. In *Souvenirs sur l'Affaire*, Blum remarked that "we try to do what Jaurès has always done, namely, to move from the injustice done to an individual to social injustice more broadly."[6] It was thus Blum's commitment to the cause of Dreyfus that motivated his commitment to socialism and made him a "disciple" of Jaurès. Thadée Natanson, the editor of the *Revue Blanche*, wrote that "Blum stood before his elder [Jaurès] like a disciple, a disciple prepared to empty his mind for the pleasure of learning everything from such a teacher. . . . As long as Jaurès was alive, Léon Blum did nothing but listen to him. . . . This teacher did more than give him faith; he made him see that he had faith."[7] Like Proust, Blum was in thrall to Jaurès's "sometimes bold quixotic nature," which led him to attack injustice in all its forms.[8]

Somewhat later, in 1904, he played an important role in founding the newspaper *L'Humanité*, of which Jaurès became the editor. Other Dreyfusards, especially the Jewish sociologists Lucien Lévy-Bruhl and Marcel Mauss, also lent a hand. Mauss served for a time as a columnist. Funds were solicited from Émile Durkheim.[9] Many letters attest to Blum's crucial role in raising money and choosing journalists.[10] Along with Lucien Herr, Jules Renard, Daniel Halévy, and Anatole France, Blum became a regular contributor to *L'Humanité* as a literary critic. This newspaper, which became the voice of socialism in twentieth-century France, can thus trace its origins to militant Dreyfusard circles, which promoted the defense of universalist values, the extension of democracy, and justice based on critical reason.

Blum's brand of socialism thus derived from Jaurès's. It was a deeply original synthesis of idealism and materialism, democracy and Marxism, individualism and collectivism, the values of the French Revolution and the theory of class struggle, revolution and reform. Jaurès imagined a socialism that would respect the rule of law as well as Marx's economic laws and theory of history based on class conflict. Above all he sought compromise and rejected violence as a danger to the Republic. Unlike other French socialists, such as Jules Guesde and Édouard Vaillant, Jaurès respected republican principles, which were contested by elements of the left that denounced the exploitation of the proletariat and accused the Republic of using violence to defend the bourgeois order and repress workers. The Dreyfus Affair brought these divergences into the open. Some socialist leaders refused to join in the captain's defense: for them, the injustice done to Dreyfus had been done by the bourgeois class to one of its own. The struggle to rehabilitate the captain thus masked the essential, namely, the oppression of the working class and the misery of the people. This was the only injustice worth fighting. At the beginning of the affair Jaurès was not far from sharing this view. He seemed indifferent to the fate of the Jewish captain and even wrote articles hostile to his cause. But during the summer of 1898, he abruptly changed camp, and his belated intervention in the name of law and justice proved decisive.[11] Jaurès did not see the state purely as an instrument of class domination. Though involved in social conflict, the state was also the guarantor of law and order and as such could be expected to recognize Dreyfus's innocence.

Influenced by Kantian ideas of rational ethics and by the belief that the individual consciousness is the basis of all action and understanding, Jaurès held that "socialism is the supreme affirmation of individual rights. Nothing stands above the individual. . . . To be sure, individuals are parts of vast systems, but those systems are valid for them only to the extent they take individual interests into account." Thus communism was seen as "the supreme form and ultimate guarantee of the loftiest universal individualism."[12] For Jaurès, there was no contradiction between individualism and socialism, and the best place to reconcile the two was the Republic. This was the key point that Blum would take from his new teacher. Summarizing Jaurès's view, Blum wrote that "these two previously divergent notions [socialism and republicanism] are in fact intertwined, inextricably associated. It would therefore be difficult to say whether he was essentially republican or still more essentially socialist."[13]

Jaurès worked out his view of the world during the struggle to establish the Third Republic, which ended with the victory of Léon Gambetta and the triumph of the ideals of the French Revolution. He was a revolutionary in the spirit of 1789. In his view, the Third Republic embodied the spirit of the Revolution, which it would complete by bringing about the triumph of socialism.[14] Rejecting economic determinism, Jaurès restored the role of ideas, morality, and ethics and "did not accept Marx's view that religious, political, and moral concepts are merely reflections of economic phenomena."[15] He thus situated socialism in a national framework, rejecting abstract internationalist views that denied the relevance of national identities. He stressed the vital importance of "the indivisible fund of impressions, memories, and emotions . . . modes of thought and feeling shared by all individual members of the particular group" in which socialism hoped to thrive.[16] Although Jaurès believed in historical materialism, accepted the Marxist theory of value, and viscerally supported the cause of the proletariat, he did not hesitate to write that "Marx was wrong" because "the Republic is the political form of socialism."[17]

In France, therefore, there was no need for a dictatorship of the proletariat. The state could be conquered by peaceful means, and adopting such means was the right way to proceed.[18] For Jaurès, the advent of the new society would depend on "the extent to which each nation's regime is democratic; on the scope, intelligence, organization and efficacy of universal suffrage; and on the difficulty of mounting coups or making revolutions by accident or chance."[19] Thus reforms affecting the laws of property, income tax, pensions, and education would lead to socialism. The key point for Jaurès was this: "Universal suffrage, for all its uncertainties, errors, and surprises, is light—bright daylight. Every force is obliged to express itself through the ballot box, and every conscience is obliged to reveal itself."[20] Rejecting both the Blanquist idea of a minority coup d'état and the Guesdist adherence to the strict letter of Marxism, Jaurès did not rule out socialist participation in government and in 1899, in the midst of the Dreyfus Affair, supported socialist Alexandre Millerand's decision to join the government of Pierre Waldeck-Rousseau—a decision rejected by many socialists, including Jules Guesde and Rosa Luxemburg, who believed that class struggle was the only way forward.[21]

This was the context in which Blum took part in the Socialist Congress at Japy in December 1899, of which he wrote a colorful account. Again using "Goethe" as his mouthpiece, Blum left vivid descriptions of the main speakers at the first Socialist Congress, including Jules Guesde, Paul Brousse, Édouard Vaillant, and Jean Allemane. He made no secret of his preference for Jaurès, who, as Blum himself would do later, "spoke with a slow, simple voice that gradually swelled and rose in tone" to challenge attacks on his position in favor of socialist participation in government. Blum, at first quoting Jaurès, concludes:

> "I do not like Millerand . . . but I maintain that Millerand's action [in joining the government] was in no way in contradiction with the revolutionary concept of class struggle, indeed that it was an example of it, a model revolutionary act. When we think of revolution and revolutionary action, we naturally tend to interpret these words historically, to fill them with images, memories, and vengeful sentiments from the past. We conjure up images of Paris in flames, of barricades, of insurgents in rags eating bullets—the whole heroic and bloody iconography of the June Days and May Days. But the meaning of words evolves with practical necessities. The troops patrolling the Faubourg St.-Antoine no longer carry rifles; the National Guard has been abolished. Now our troops are equipped with automatic weapons and rapid-fire cannons. Prefect Haussmann cut broad streets through the heart of Paris and Prefect Poubelle paved them with wood that crumbled easily and therefore could not be used for barricades. I do not know what future revolutions will look like, but it is certain that they will be different from the revolutions of the past. Yet revolutionary acts are still possible. What kind? I, for one, will continue to apply the term to any act that seems to me to accelerate the regular course of political evolution. . . . In this sense, there can be no doubt that Millerand's participation in a bourgeois government was in itself a revolutionary act." . . . Jaurès was the first politician to recognize the significance of the Dreyfus

Affair, a man whose civic courage, availing itself of the power of truth, impressed the popular masses with his moral superiority.[22]

This essay, written in January 1900, was a harbinger of Blum's own approach to politics, which would lead to the victory of the Popular Front in 1936—a victory based on a broad coalition that would include the Radical Party. Although Blum made some use of revolutionary Marxist rhetoric, he was more explicit than Jaurès in advocating reformist socialism, which grew out of the "*normalien* socialism" associated with the Dreyfus Affair and focused on improving the condition of the working class.[23] Blum's socialism was influenced by his interaction with Jewish sociologists such as Émile Durkheim and Marcel Mauss, both admirers of the French Revolution and critics of Marxism and Bolshevism. Both men were close to Jaurès, and both stressed in their work the importance of collective representations for achieving social cohesion and fashioning a collective national identity. Blum was thus one of a group of Jewish *normaliens* who joined the socialist cause.[24] He implicitly subscribed to a French version of revisionism largely conceived by Lucien Herr, whom he remained quite close to, as we know from countless personal letters that reveal the profound intimacy of their relationship.[25] By the turn of the century, Blum believed that "among thinking socialists, no one is unaware that Marx's metaphysics is mediocre or that another link in his chain of economic arguments breaks every day."[26] He also rejected dramatic conceptions of history and the heroic metaphysics of revolution. Like Jaurès but without Jaurès's hesitations, Blum laid the groundwork for seeing reformist strategy as a revolutionary approach suited to contemporary conditions.

In 1902, Jaurès became the head of a French Socialist Party that rejected any form of revisionism or participation in government as incompatible with class struggle, although it approved Millerand's participation in Waldeck-Rousseau's "government of republican defense" in 1899 as an exceptional experiment. Blum immediately embraced this strategy but remained aloof from discussions of policy and ideology. In 1905, he joined without much enthusiasm a new socialist formation that unified all the rival factions: the Section Française de l'Internationale Ouvrière (SFIO), which accepted the Guesdist refusal to compromise even though Jaurès was its most prominent personality. Blum chose to stay out of a debate that he felt was incompatible with the views of his teacher. Instead, he devoted more time to his work as a literary critic.

History overtook him, however. On July 31, 1914, Jaurès was assassinated by a rabid nationalist. A profoundly shaken Blum accepted a position as chief of staff to Marcel Sembat, a socialist minister in the "Union Sacrée" (wartime coalition government), the first government to which the Socialist Party gave its full assent. On July 31, 1917, Blum wrote an article for *L'Humanité* to commemorate the third anniversary of Jaurès's assassination, with the intent of perpetuating the slain leader's ideas.[27] Like Jaurès, Blum believed that the conditions of revolution had changed profoundly, particularly in light of the Bolshevik Revolution. In statement after statement Blum insisted that armed rebellion was outmoded because of the sophisticated weaponry available to the modern state. In a lecture on Jaurès that same month, he noted that his late mentor had "understood, and I believe he was the first to understand, that in the current state of society, certain reforms are tantamount to revolution . . . [and] that now and in the future, revolution is not and will not be an affair of barricades, insurgents eating bullets, conspiracies, or coups led by secret societies. On the contrary, a revolutionary act occurs . . . each time the working class achieves significant progress sooner than would have been the case in the normal course of events. . . . Reform is revolutionary, and revolution is reformist." Staunchly opposed to "sublime messianism," Blum followed in the footsteps of Jaurès, calling for a reformist revolution, for action within the framework of bourgeois society—a compromise between socialism and the Republic. In his eyes, Jaurès was a man of "faith." His "sanctity" combined "religious emotion" with "rational intelligence." Socialism represented the "harmonious" culmination of "Greek philosophy, Jewish prophecy, and Christian morality."[28]

In 1906, Jaurès had proposed that Blum run for election as deputy, but Blum chose not to take up the offer. His speech to the special Socialist Party congress in 1919, one year before the important Congress of Tours, revealed how similar Blum's view of politics was to his teacher's. Blum's speech was filled with Marxist language regarding the fate of the proletariat, the transformation of property, and the injustice and contradictions of capitalism, but the real gist of the speech lay in the claim that "the proletarian revolution . . . will not be opposed in any way to the idea of democracy or the democratic ideal."[29] Like Jaurès, Blum hoped that the proletariat would take power by legal means, that is, by winning a parliamentary majority and respecting existing state institutions. He outlined a theory of power that differed in every way from the Bolshevik strategy, which had gained considerable influence among French Socialists. In opposition to the party's right wing, which was urging him to choose between Woodrow Wilson and democracy on one hand and Lenin and Bolshevik fanaticism on the other, Blum replied: "I choose neither Wilson nor Lenin but Jaurès. We will remain revolutionary socialists without in any way succumbing to the influence of the Bolsheviks."[30]

In November 1919, Blum was elected for the first time as deputy for Paris. Eventually he rose to become head of the Socialist Party. The positions he took on issues followed directly from those Jaurès had taken before him, but Blum had the opportunity to put his teacher's ideas into practice as a duly elected representative of the nation. In July 1920, a short while after his election and after the Bolshevik victory in Russia and the birth of the Third International, Blum wrote several articles for *L'Humanité* in which he denounced a strategy based on a revolutionary "avant-garde maintaining strict homogeneity in its ranks through purges and subject to a rigid and partly secret hierarchy culminating in an executive committee in Moscow." Such submission to foreign authority would have shocked the patriotic and internationalist Jaurès. In solidarity with the class struggle in other countries, Blum also rejected any form of internationalism that failed to do justice to national identities. In the words of the Socialist Charles Rapoport, he opposed the kind of "Blanquism with tartar sauce" that sought to impose the Bolshevik strategy on other nations. In Blum's view, the Bolsheviks "forget that in France and other Western countries, power can be obtained only by vast workers' movements like the one in England, movements that involve not masses of unorganized proletarians but millions of organized workers working consciously toward a clearly defined goal."[31] In France, the laws of the Republic established a framework within which socialism could come to power while respecting individual liberties.

Blum unwaveringly accepted Jaurès's Kantianism, his appeal to reason, and his belief that the consciousness of the individual was the engine of social change. On this basis he honed the arguments he would use at the Congress of Tours, which ended in the historic separation of socialism and communism.[32] The Bolsheviks had set up the Third International to demand absolute obedience from the new communist parties in other countries, which were expected to accept twenty-one conditions, including adherence to all decisions made in Moscow notwithstanding differences of local conditions and political traditions (such as the existence of parliamentary democracy). Foreign parties could join the Third International only if they agreed to a strategy of violent seizure of power and accepted the dominant role of the Communist Party in achieving a dictatorship of the proletariat. Iron discipline was to be the rule, and no internal dissidence or minority faction could be tolerated. Trade unions had to be subordinate to the party, and reformism was denounced as treason tantamount to submission to bourgeois domination. As the fatherland of socialism, Bolshevik Russia had to be defended in every instance, even in defiance of national interests.

In a declaration dated July 26, 1920, and signed by Lenin and Grigory Zinoviev, the executive committee of the Communist International vehemently attacked the SFIO, denouncing its leaders as "valets of the bourgeoisie" and "social patriots" preoccupied with "parliamentary trivialities." Zinoviev demanded "a clean break with the reformist tradition" and denounced the socialism of Jaurès, calling on the new party to reject it.[33] Many motions were filed, including one signed by Blum, who rejected the idea of centralized decision-making and exclusion of minorities, insisted on free and open debate, and accepted the class struggle but without ruling out legal and parliamentary action while insisting that the dictatorship of the proletariat could only be temporary.[34] Contradicting Lenin, Blum published another text in his capacity as secretary of the Socialist group in parliament, boldly defending his actions as being in the interest of the working class.[35] Public debate began on December 25, 1920, with Ludovic-Oscar Frossard defending the party's adherence to the Third International, which the majority supported. Other party leaders followed him to the podium. Marcel Sembat, whom Blum had served as chief of staff during World War I, proclaimed that "the truth according to Jaurès, the truth as he taught it to us, is the opposite of the truth from Moscow."[36]

On December 27, 1920, Blum took the floor at a dramatic moment, as the two hostile factions of the SFIO were about to make their split permanent. He spoke at length in a highly charged atmosphere, brushing aside interruptions and insults. The courage and loftiness of his speech left an indelible mark on those who heard it. Once again, Blum denounced Bolshevik-style socialism:

> What kind of new party do you want to create? Instead of a party in which the popular will is formed at the base and filters up by degrees, your centralized regime subordinates each level to the next higher level of the hierarchy. . . . All the Moscow debates anticipate a complete and radical purge of everything the Socialist Party is now. . . . Anyone who votes against adhesion and does not submit entirely to the new order will be eliminated from the Third International.[37]

Blum opposed the strategy of an armed seizure of power by "a secret society, a sort of vast conspiracy of *carbonari*," or disciplined minority. He ironically dismissed Lenin's ideas as ill-adapted to France: "That is how you see things. What did the Blanquists achieve with such a strategy? Not much. . . . In recent years they haven't been able to seize so much as a fire station on the Boulevard de la Villette."[38] Blum rejected any form of undemocratic minority action. In his view, the "unorganized masses" were only too ripe to be enlisted in "sheeplike violence," supporting now Clemenceau, now a dangerous adventurist like General Boulanger. Although it was true that in the West reformism without seizure of power had proved incapable of changing the status of property, and although he did not share the reformist position of Édouard Bernstein, Blum also believed that "the anarchist error that . . . is at the root of the communist doctrine" could be reduced to the idea that the state could simply be seized by force.[39] He rejected both Bolshevism and reformism and, following Jaurès, showed that although revolution as he conceived it did involve a moment of "discontinuity," that moment had to be preceded by "gradual changes" achieved by legal as well as illegal means. Although a dictatorship of the proletariat exercised by a party on behalf of the masses could be tolerated, a dictatorship "exercised by a party organized as ours is, and not yours" could only be "temporary and provisional" and must not be reduced to "a dictatorship of a few individuals. . . . That is the Moscow system. . . . You conceive of terrorism not only as an ultimate recourse, not as an extreme measure of public safety that you would adopt to overcome bourgeois resistance, not as a vital necessity for the revolution, but as a means of government."[40] Faced with the rising strength of international communism, which a broad segment of the anti-revisionist socialist movement in France embraced, Blum, speaking at a historic party congress in which Bolshevik influence was strong, conceded the potential need for a temporary dictatorship of the proletariat: "We favor it. . . . We favor the theory of the dictatorship of the proletariat so strongly that we included it in our party's campaign platform."[41] Blum thus accepted the need for a transitional dictatorship of the proletariat but paradoxically believed that it could be achieved by legal means, including free democratic elections as advocated by Jaurès.

Blum anticipated that he would be in the minority at Tours and be excluded from the movement because he refused to accept the conditions of the Third International, and he knew this would lead to a durable schism in the French socialist movement. The moving finale to his speech is remembered to this day: "While you court adventure, someone has to keep watch over the old house."[42] His hope was to keep the SFIO alive until the moment was more propitious for a Jaurès-style socialism, a socialism informed by the Enlightenment and the universalist heritage of the French Revolution—in a word, republican socialism.

No sooner had he finished speaking, however, than one delegate rose to accuse him of "confusionism," while another proclaimed: "We knew that Citizen Léon Blum was the leader of those who seek to destroy the unity of the party. . . . It is impossible for truly revolutionary socialists to be in the same party as Léon Blum."[43] A few minutes later, Charles Rappoport, who favored affiliation with the Third International, declared that "the Bolshevik Party emerged from the fight against class collaboration and against the tactics of Bernstein, a respectable theorist, no less respectable than Blum but also no less opportunistic."[44] As the time for the vote that would seal the break in the party drew near, Karl Marx's grandson Jean Longuet ended his speech with these words: "Our comrade Blum said that while some of us would seek adventure, we ought to watch over the old house. I beg you, if we want to keep the old house, let's all stay in it. Let's not quit our party to join a new Communist Party that will no longer be the party of Jaurès. . . . The fanaticism that Jaurès so eloquently decried must be opposed. The jeers of the fanatics must be confronted. . . . The moment has come for you to decide if you're ready to submit to the knout. I, for one, am not."[45]

During his lengthy intervention, whose historic importance everyone recognized, Blum implicitly set himself up as a rival to Lenin and Trotsky. It was a decisive step, which made him the leader of the non-communist socialists, independent of Moscow and unwilling to submit to any extra-national power, to any authority other than that of the Republic and any tradition other than the universalist tradition of the Enlightenment. To be sure, his action continued to reflect the influence of Jaurès, but by December 1920, the die was cast and schism was inevitable. The minority faction, followers of Blum, Paul Faure, and Jean Longuet, retained the name SFIO and the battle cry "Vive Jaurès!" Rejecting both reformist ideology and armed revolution, the SFIO was considerably weakened by the departure of the majority, which joined the new Communist Party and accepted most of the harsh conditions laid down by the Third International. In the eyes of the world, Léon Blum now symbolized a distinctly French path to socialism, at once peaceful and revolutionary.

Two years after the Congress of Tours, Blum reiterated his deep disagreement with Bolshevism in the clearest of terms. For him, the dictatorship of the proletariat could not be a "sect" or a "dictatorship *over* the proletariat." It would "have to honor freedom of thought, freedom of assembly, freedom of discussion. . . . Every individual should be allowed to participate . . . in democratic activity more spontaneous and intense than ever."[46] In 1922, Blum again invoked the legacy of Lucien Herr and Jean Jaurès in advocating equality through "reason and justice" and a socialism that "will improve the condition of women, children, emotional life, and family life." He called for profound social change, for a revolution "that can be achieved by legal means, through a victory of universal suffrage."[47] This was his strongest statement to date against the Bolshevist course chosen by the majority. In speech after speech and article after article in *Le Populaire* (*L'Humanité* having fallen into the hands of the Communist Party), he invoked the spirit of Jaurès to denounce the Bolshevik strategy of an "armed coup" led by "perpetually mobilized shock troops, a sort of professional army of insurrection" that did not shrink from "the most atrocious cruelty . . . including torture of unarmed and helpless adversaries, forever tainting the first great proletarian victories with stains of horror and blood as indelible as those on the hands of Lady Macbeth."[48]

Blum's warnings drew little response from intellectuals fascinated by the radicalism of the Bolshevik revolution, who now saw him as a lackey of the bourgeoisie, a social traitor to be fought if not killed. Yet his analysis, dating from the 1920s, of the "cruelty" to which the centralist, authoritarian logic of Bolshevism infallibly leads attests to his prescience. It preceded the testimony of Victor Kravchenko, Arthur Koestler, and Alexander Solzhenitsyn by decades and remains today one of the most impressive exposés of the logic of totalitarianism.

Blum never forgot his debt to Jaurès. He worked hard to persuade the socialist rank and file of the rightness of Jaurès's views in the French context. He also remained active in the Socialist Second International, which rejected the Bolshevist strategy of the Leninist Third International. On July 31 of every year, the anniversary of Jaurès's assassination, Blum delivered a memorial speech. On several occasions he inaugurated streets named for Jaurès, expressing pleasure in the reverence shown to his hero: "Today and forever after, it is essential that workers preserve the memory of Jean Jaurès and share in his joys, his celebrations, his struggles, and his sorrows. . . . It is we who need this faith, not Jaurès. . . . Jaurès had confidence in the collective soul, the popular soul. And he knew that his confidence would never be disappointed."[49] In November 1924, Jaurès's coffin was transferred from Albi to the Panthéon in Paris. A procession consisting of a hearse preceded by a group of miners and followed by the entire government, a contingent of high civil servants, students from the École Normale Supérieure, members of the Socialist Party and Ligue des Droits de l'Homme, and union militants, made its way across Paris as nearly half a million spectators looked on.[50] Blum noted that "the entire nation has joined us in mourning and I dare say in devotion. Jaurès's mortal remains have come to take their place in the Panthéon, alongside the great heroes of the Revolution and the Republic. . . . Watched over by the miners of Carmaux . . . escorted by them, his body has made its way across Paris before the eyes of a multitude, as Gambetta's body did long ago. . . . By recognizing Jaurès's immortality, the nation has acknowledged that it often underestimated or ignored him during his lifetime."[51]

In 1930 Blum taught at the Socialist School a course on "Jaurès and the intellectuals" in which he showed how Jaurès had won the Dreyfusard intellectuals over to the social-ist cause.[52] In February 1933 he gave a lecture at the Théâtre des Ambassadeurs in Paris: "This was a man I loved, a man in whose shadow I lived for the last sixteen or seventeen years of his life, and whom I greeted at the Gare du Nord two days before his death." He insisted on Jaurès's "genius" and never-ending "quest for a just society, a harmonious society capable of joining . . . the laws of collective prosperity with those of individual happiness."[53] He again pointed out the crucial role Jaurès had played in the Dreyfus Affair, his determination to see that justice was done, and his vision of a socialism that "does not call for violence, indeed his ardent wish that victory could be achieved without it."

Socialism, Blum insisted, was the challenge posed by "the vast majority of humankind, the proletarians," to the power of an oligarchy. The victory of socialism need not take the form "recorded in literature and color prints of insurgents on barricades facing a hail of bullets."[54] As he prepared to lead a vast coalition to victory at the polls, Blum, to the end faith-ful to Jaurès, once again questioned, in the same terms as be-fore, the imagery of revolution he rejected, the imagery of the Blanquists of old and the Bolsheviks of the present, who had built it into the official program of the Communist Party, with which it would henceforth be necessary to reach an accom-modation.[55] In 1938, Geoffrey Fraser and Thadée Natanson, who had known Jaurès well, wrote: "It is a tragic thought that Jaurès, like Moses of old, died before entering the Promised Land, and that it was not given to him to know that it would be the young man whom he had loved and trained who was to have that honor."[56] Blum liked this conceit linking socialism to Judaism so well that he made it his own.[57]

5

In Service of the State

DURING HIS long march to power, Blum had the opportunity to acquire the kind of solid legal background essential for
mastering the apparatus of government. Some of the state Jews
like him served in the prefectural corps and the judiciary, while
others climbed the ranks of the military. Only the cream of
the crop entered the sanctum sanctorum: the Council of State,
France's highest administrative law body. After being expelled
from the École Normale Supérieure for poor attendance, Blum
earned degrees in literature and law, from the Sorbonne and
the Paris Law Faculty, before taking the Council's entrance ex-
amination. After failing on his first try, he succeeded on the
second and was named an *auditeur*, a civil servant in charge of
cases brought before the Council of State, in January 1896, and
thereafter he rose slowly through the ranks. In this prestigious
institution he met other state Jews, such as André Spire and
Paul Grunebaum-Ballin, who became a close friend. He and

Blum moved in the same social circles, frequented the same salons, and knew both Proust and Jaurès.

Blum's career with the Council lasted more than twenty
years. In 1907 he was promoted to *maître des requêtes* (master
of appeals), and in 1910 he became a *commissaire* (whose written legal interpretations often become part of permanent case
law). Later, when he was elected to Parliament in November
1919, he was forced to resign from his Council post.[1] To borrow a curious term used in the *New Conversations of Goethe
with Eckermann*, Blum "insinuated" himself into the Council
of State by proving himself an energetic and effective civil servant. Though a specialist in administrative law, he nevertheless
accepted the socialist view of the state as an instrument of the
bourgeoisie. Like a schizophrenic, he filled two contradictory
roles at once, as both servant of the state and adept of socialist
revolution.[2] In the same youthful work he argued that "only in
a centralized, unified, leveled nation are individuals truly liberated. The Montagnards of 1793 saw this, but the Girondins
whom Barrès invokes did not."[3] Like all French Jews at the
time, he deeply admired the French Revolution, which had
separated the state from the Catholic Church and allowed it
to play an emancipatory role. The state became the scourge of
particularisms of every kind and guaranteed every individual
equal access to public space. On this view, the centralized state
is a more powerful agent of individual liberation than social
revolution. Moreover, the action of the state is determined by
a logic of its own that cannot be reduced to class relations.

Blum continued to adhere to this view throughout his life.
On May 10, 1936, for example, after winning an election, he
said this to party delegates gathered in the grand ballroom of
the Hôtel Moderne:

> As I have said repeatedly, we want to use the state and will
> use it to intervene in all the nerve centers of the economy in

order to revitalize it, to infuse it with the energy a convalescent feels when he ventures outdoors for the first time and feels the blood once again flowing in his veins.

As he assumed power, in his speech to Parliament he was careful to assure the deputies that "we will govern as republicans. We will uphold the republican order. We will firmly enforce the law in defense of the republic. We will demonstrate that our aim is to infuse all the agencies and departments of government with the republican spirit."[4] By "republican order" he meant the state created by the French Revolution and not a government of the proletariat out to do away with bourgeois society. The republican state was one that acted in accordance with its own internal logic. At a moment of profound historic change, Blum sought to reassure the public on this point. Speaking on May 31 at the Salle Huygens, he insisted that "there is no proletarian majority. There is a majority for the Popular Front, for which the Popular Front program is the center of gravity. Our purpose, our mandate, our platform is to carry out and complete this program. It follows that we will act within the limits of the existing social regime, the very regime whose contradictions and injustice we demonstrated in our campaign." Unambiguously, he continued: "We will operate entirely legally, within the framework of existing institutions, of society as currently constituted, and of the existing property regime. . . . The public good is our sole purpose. We are, in the noblest sense of the word, a national government."[5]

Blum thus shared a conception of the state common to other *normalien* socialists, such as Émile Durkheim, who saw the state as an organ of thought, an agent of Reason arising from the organic division of labor. This was a quasi-Hegelian vision of the state, according to which civil servants are neutral agents of the public good.[6] It was also close to the view of Jaurès, who saw the state as an autonomous power: "In a democracy the state is not exclusively a class state and will become less and less so," a view diametrically opposed to the Marxist understanding.[7] In *À l'échelle humaine* (On the Human Scale), Blum argued that "the power of the state should be used to define, protect, and guarantee the condition of the working class."[8] In 1947, he insisted that "capitalism today no longer exerts mastery over the democratic state."[9] In the great tradition of state Jews, Blum thus saw the state historically as an instrument of emancipation and not merely the secular arm of the bourgeoisie, which, according to Marx and Engels, would inevitably resort to violence before withering away when class conflict finally came to an end. In his final, emotional homage to Jaurès, delivered in May 1947 at the École Normale Supérieure, where both men had studied, Blum forcefully argued:

> In most European countries, the state is no longer purely and simply an instrument or exact reflection of capitalism. . . . The modern state gradually detached itself from capitalism, and that is why socialist parties are able to make use of it without conquering it or becoming subservient to capitalism. In taking power they use the state as an instrument to fight against capitalism, employing the authority of the state to create conditions favorable to the advent of socialism.[10]

Spanning a period of many years, these texts attest to a vision of the state quite different from that of the Third International and the French Communist Party. It is the vision of a high civil servant and longtime official of the Council of State, a man devoted to the idea of public service who spent his career in administrative law. Blum served as *rapporteur*, writing the case law interpretations, in 266 cases, and between 1902 and 1919 he drafted 1,800 opinions. Unfortunately, nearly all of these have disappeared, but the sheer number of cases he was involved in tells us what an important role he played in this most prestigious of French administrative institutions.[11] Blum sought to reinforce the role of the state and strengthen its hand in the administration of municipalities and public services, and even in the regulation of industry and commerce. In an important case known as *Époux Lemonnier*, decided in July 1918, he broke new legal ground by demonstrating that responsibility rested not only with the mayor of a town but with the town itself as part of the larger French state. In this case, a mayor was held responsible for negligence in the death of an individual, but Blum argued that the state was also at fault. In Blum's eminent words, "the administrative judge can and must say: 'The fault may be separable from the service. It is up to the [civil] courts to decide. But the service cannot be separated from the fault.'" In this and other renowned judgments, Blum helped create a sense of solidarity in regard to administrative risk, thus making common cause with "Solidarists" such as the philosopher Léon Bourgeois and the sociologist Célestin Bouglé, whom he met in connection with his work on the Dreyfus Affair, as well as the legal theorist Léon Duguit. Like Duguit, Blum saw the state as an animating presence: it was not a dominant power but a manager of public services and thus an agent of citizen solidarity.[12]

His opinion in *Compagnie générale française des tramways* (March 1910) was similar: the state was responsible for the operation of a tram line run by a private firm in the public interest. This decision was crucial because it held, again to Duguit's satisfaction, that private railway companies remain subject to "the sovereignty, command, and *imperium* of the state." As Blum pointed out to the Chamber of Deputies (the lower house of Parliament) in 1927, "the Government derives from its prerogatives as a public power, from its command authority over firms, and from its national and legislative sovereignty" the right to impose its will on private companies.[13] The general thrust of Blum's decisions is clear: he placed the state at the heart of social and economic life. For Georges Vedel, "the chief characteristic of Léon Blum's work as a government commissioner was to see the state as a public service, an agency providing services rather than exercising sovereignty."[14] He thereby strengthened the role of the state, interpreting it as an instrument of the general interest and of socialism even though it did nothing to alter the capitalist structure of society. "Blum's socialism developed a critique of the state independent of Marxism. . . . His socialism reserved a crucial place for the state."[15] His role in the evolution of case law at the Council of State should therefore not be underestimated. As another state Jew employed by the same institution observed, Blum "dedicated his brilliant mind, unrivaled culture, and prodigious gifts to the Council for more than twenty years, and proved himself a master of the arts of exposition and analysis as litigator, rapporteur, and commissioner. . . . With his brilliance as an individual and the quality of his work, no one contributed more to the Council than he."[16]

Blum put his idea of the state into practice as chief of Marcel Sembat's staff during World War I. Knowing the ropes of the administration, he had an insider's understanding of how the French government worked and how a centralized but far-flung apparatus could shape society. He distilled his experience in *La réforme gouvernementale* (Governmental Reform, first published in 1918), a book based on his wartime work in government. In it he argued for strengthening parliamentary democracy and for using political parties as instruments of the national will. He hoped this would lead, as in Great Britain, to an organized and disciplined party system that would afford the prime minister great latitude. The executive, in his view, should be "a monarch . . . a temporary monarch who can be dismissed at any time but who wields full executive power as long as Parliament allows."[17] While concerned to preserve a democratic regime in which the parties played a key role, Blum nevertheless argued that the executive should be the linchpin of political action and went so far as to condemn the principle of separation of powers. In his view, the prime minister was to be "the guide, the arbiter," the uncontested leader of the parliamentary majority. He was to occupy "his high command post. . . . The practical means of command have not changed since Louis XIV"—that is, since the king famously declared "l'état, c'est moi."[18]

Blum proposed to repair the defects of the French parliamentary system, with its fragile and fickle majorities, by creating a limited cabinet consisting mainly of high civil servants as permanent members alongside temporary members selected by the "leader." Such a reform, he believed, would prove as decisive as the creation of the Council of State by Napoleon. He derided the École Libre des Sciences Politiques (School of Political Science) created by Hippolyte Taine and Émile Boutmy. In his view, this school did little more than prepare students to pass certain administrative exams. It was not a training ground for future ministers, and in the spirit of Blum's reform, ministers were not in any case to be drawn from the civil service. He argued that "governing is in the final analysis administering with a political goal in mind. Having some knowledge of our high civil servants, I would not trust them to choose such a goal."[19] In Blum's plan, the democratically elected party leader who became prime minister would rely on ministers drawn from the Chamber of Deputies, ministers who shared his values and who would govern in conjunction with the civil servants in the cabinet. Above all, the prime minister should be able to count on the support of a competent and apolitical civil service. Blum's reform thus drew on a tradition of statecraft derived from Louis XIV and Napoleon, the leaders who built the centralized French state with its powerful bureaucracy, but he combined this with a role for politics in the selection of ministers from the parliamentary majority.[20]

In many respects Blum's reform proposals were inspired by the example of Great Britain, with its all-powerful cabinet backed by a parliamentary majority. In France, however, the alliance of parliament and cabinet took on a very different meaning, because the state, far from being weak as in Britain, was highly institutionalized and differentiated. Both Tocqueville and Marx (in his analysis of Bonapartism) stressed the exceptional character of the French state, its ability to rise above social conflict and act according to its own internal logic, thus leaving its stamp on society. The cleverness of Blum's proposal lay in the way it combined a technocratic vision of "a well-regulated machine" with a socialist policy backed by a parliamentary majority.[21] Aware of the peculiarities of the French state, with its relative insulation from political, social, and religious forces, Blum was the first of a new type of state Jew interested in giving greater weight to democratic sentiment within the framework of a socialist project.[22] It was by no means obvious that such contradictory visions could be reconciled, the logic of the state having little in common with that of class struggle or even democracy.

In order to resolve this contradiction, Blum set forth an important distinction between "the exercise of state power" and "the conquest of state power." The latter was a remote goal, to be sought only after social harmony was achieved and the state had all but disappeared, whereas the mere exercise of state power within existing legal institutions could be done immediately. Blum thus envisioned a middle road between mere reformism and a Bolshevik-style seizure of power. In the era of the Cartel des Gauches (Coalition of the Left), led by Édouard Herriot's Radical Party and supported by the Socialists in 1924, Blum was led to spell out the socialist attitude toward power more precisely. Under his impetus, the Socialists voted to support the Radicals, whose program of social and economic reform was not very different from theirs. In January 1926, following the collapse of the Cartel, Blum formulated his distinction between the exercise and conquest of power for the first time. At the so-called Bellevilloise Congress of the Socialist Party he said this:

Although I am not a legalist when it comes to the conquest of power, I am one when it comes to the exercise of power. If parliamentary processes result in our being called upon to exercise power within the framework of existing institutions, we should do so legally and fairly without taking advantage of our presence in government to fraudulently transform the exercise of power into the conquest of power.[23]

Blum thus tried to move beyond mere support for the government without actual participation in the exercise of power. This shift in stance would lead within a few years to the Popular Front. His position was clear: if the Socialist Party came to power, it would abide by the rules. The question would soon become urgent, owing to the rise of fascism, of the "Hitlerian racists" whose actions Blum tirelessly attacked in the Chamber, along with the mobilization of the extreme right in France, which posed a threat to democracy.[24]

In 1934, many politicians were caught up in the Stavisky Affair.[25] After the swindler Alexandre Stavisky committed suicide, it became clear that many officials had afforded him protection from the law. The right-wing party Action Française mounted protests, in which it was joined by forces from Solidarité Française, the Croix de Feu, and other vehemently nationalist, anti-Semitic groups. On February 6, 1934, tens of thousands of demonstrators attempted to seize the National Assembly, or Parliament. These groups published tracts denouncing various political leaders. Solidarité Française distributed one that read as follows:

> Daladier is leading you like sheep to the slaughter run by the Blums, Kaisersteins, Schweinkopfs, and Zyromskis of the world, whose very French names speak volumes about their goals.
>
> These are your masters, patriots!
> France must belong to the French
> And the French must feel at home in France.[26]

Faced with an attempted coup, the police fired on the crowd, killing fifteen people and wounding two thousand. Blum courageously remained in his seat in the Chamber, even though many deputies deserted their posts rather than confront the violence. Blum went to the podium, lashed out at the rioters, warmly defended the Republic, and alone implored Daladier not to resign.[27] Years later Blum wrote that in view of the fascist threat, which prefigured "the cowardly terror of Vichy," and feeling personally threatened both as leader of the socialist movement and as a Jew, he approached the Communist Party, which in accord with Moscow had changed strategy and now sought a national union to counter the danger of Hitler while putting its own revolutionary ambitions on hold.[28] On February 12, socialists and communists joined in a vast protest march against the attempted right-wing coup—a march that anticipated the success of the Popular Front two years later. Here is Blum's account of that historic day, which brought together marchers from the two rival parties.

> It was to defend the Republic, to preserve the essence of the Republic, that we would have transcended the bounds of republican law if necessary. . . . We moved forward. The interval between the leading elements of the two columns of marchers decreased every second, and each of us felt the same anxiety. Would the encounter lead to a clash? . . . I was too responsible for the events of that day not to feel deeply emotional. The two columns now stood face to face, and identical shouts broke out on all sides. Identical songs were sung. The two columns came together, but there was no clash, only fraternization.[29]

Conditions were now ripe for an alliance of the forces of the left to lead the government. In July 1935, when the moment came to announce the Common Program of the Left, Blum returned to the question of power. In these exceptional circumstances, with fascism on the march abroad and the extreme right on the move in France, it was time for a "Popular Front" that would unite the parties of the left against fascism. Blum remained vague about respecting legality.[30] Once power was achieved, sweeping economic and social reform would become possible. The program of the left would be different in every way from the corporatist fascism of neo-socialists like Marcel Déat, who envisaged an authoritarian system of planning that, with its anti-democratic implications, "terrified" Blum.[31]

After World War II, with fascism no longer a threat, Blum delivered a lecture at the École Normale Supérieure in which he returned once again to the distinction between the exercise and the conquest of power. He titled his talk "The Exercise and Conquest of Power." After invoking yet again the memory of Lucien Herr and Jean Jaurès, he said that "the normal case is the exercise of power. . . . If we take part in government, we exercise power. . . . We then have to manage the society entrusted to our care honestly and fairly. That is our duty as wielders of power. But we are also socialists, and our actions should be directed toward social transformation."[32] Blum faced this contradiction by arguing that "the modern state gradually detached itself from capitalism, and that is why socialist parties are able to make use of it without conquering it or becoming subservient to capitalism."[33] In other words, what makes it possible to resolve the contradiction is the nature of the modern state, especially in France, where the state is strong and centralized. Blum's experience as a high civil servant taught him that the French state could serve as an instrument of equality and social reform. It was as if the conquest of power ceased to be anything other than its mere exercise. In the end, despite all the lyrical paeans to the French Revolution and the subtle distinctions laid before impassioned delegates at party congresses hostile to any form of compromise, Blum saw the French state as an agent of emancipation and an ideal instrument of social transformation.

6

The Attack

On February 13, 1936, Blum left the Chamber of Deputies
and joined Georges Monnet and his wife Germaine in Monnet's automobile. At the intersection of the Rue de l'Université
and the Boulevard Saint-Germain, the three found themselves
suddenly face-to-face with a large crowd of youths, students,
and Camelots du Roi (members of the youth wing of the extreme-right Action Française), who had gathered to mark the
death of the royalist historian Jacques Bainville, one of the
most vitriolic of the *Action Française* writers. As Monnet tried
to inch the car forward through the crowd, some of the demonstrators noticed Blum sitting in the back seat. Immediately,
hostile cries broke out, insults were hurled at the car, and many
of the youths made threatening gestures. The demonstrators
mobbed the automobile and hammered it with fists and canes.
Some screamed "Blum murderer!" Death threats were uttered.
An amateur filmmaker immortalized the scene as one of the

demonstrators began to beat Blum.[1] Germaine Monnet tried in vain to protect him. Wounded in the face, he bled profusely. *Le Populaire* published a description of the extremely violent attack. Louis Courtois, the aggressor,

> advanced . . . threatening, furious, screaming, holding an ignition harness in his hand. After smashing the car's window, he savagely beat the editor of this newspaper. . . . The sight of M. Blum soaked in blood only increased the frenzy of the Action Française demonstrators, and what ensued in the middle of the boulevard was a scene of revolting savagery and atrocity. Some of the Camelots kicked Blum in the stomach, while others tried to throw him to the ground and would no doubt have stomped him to death had they succeeded. "Kill Blum! Kill Blum!" they screamed.[2]

Blum was drenched in blood. The police tried to protect the Socialist leader and his friends. The Camelots smashed the rear window of the car and manhandled and beat its occupants. When the police tried to ward off the attackers, they were assisted by workers who had rushed to Blum's aid and helped him to safety in the offices of the Ligue Catholique Féminine, after the concierge of the building next door hastily locked the carriage gate to prevent them from taking refuge there.

The attack took place shortly before the election that brought the Popular Front to power, and tensions were running high. Hatred of Blum was at a fever pitch. After being treated at the Hôtel-Dieu, he issued a statement: "I now know what lynching means." With a bandage wrapped around his head, he looked like a wounded soldier from World War I. Photos portrayed him as a suffering victim rather than a hero who had courageously confronted the royalist hordes. Even in torment, Dreyfus had always managed to project an image of ramrod toughness, as befits a soldier. Once again, the images of the two men in their darkest moments seemed to stand in sharp contrast. Yet Blum had demonstrated real physical courage during the attack, just as he had done in his duels. He had tried to defend himself by protecting his body, had endured his attackers' blows in silence, and though seriously wounded had maintained his composure throughout the ordeal. As Mme Monnet recalled, "within seconds he was covered with blood, and the blows continued to fall. 'My poor friend,' I said, to which he calmly replied, 'Don't worry. Let them do what they will.'"[3] A few months later, he ironically alluded to "the little scrape I got into on the Boulevard Saint-Germain."[4] To Eugène Montel he sent the following telegram: "Minor wounds. Do not worry on my account. Urge comrades to control their emotions."[5]

Le Populaire published a long article by Bracke (Alexandre-Marie Desrousseaux) titled "They Got Him! They Almost Had Him!" which speaks volumes about the violence of the attack: "Dear Léon Blum, Sympathy and love for you pour out from those who are close to you, who know you, who admire in you even more than the marvels of your mind, and no less than your limitless devotion to what you know to be truth and justice, the calm courage and quiet firmness we witnessed today."[6] The same newspaper compared the attack on Blum to the assassination of Jaurès by Raoul Vilain. Blum received many letters praising his courage. The writer Jean-Richard Bloch had this to say:

> The wireless brings news of the abominable assault of which you were today the victim. Your courage has long been a target of their hostility, your nobility was an affront to their vileness, your independence an insult to their cowardice and servitude. I thank fortune that their blows did not achieve the hoped-for result, for which they howl their dreadful howls every morning.[7]

The philosopher Alain (Émile-Auguste Chartier) wrote these indignant lines:

My dear Blum, So this is how they reward the friend of the people and of justice. . . . So this is your reward for giving up literature, as you knew it would be. I agree with you that it is better to live as a man. But these natural reflections do not detract in the slightest from the deep indignation I want you to know I feel, even as I resolve in my own mind to avoid all the traps of moderation.[8]

Two years later, Blum received the following letter from a sympathizer:

Today, February 13, I take the liberty of writing to assure you of my deep and sympathetic admiration. I have not forgotten the day in 1936 when I sat in anguish in front of the wireless awaiting further details. At first we heard only that you had been struck, but little by little we learned all the details of the attack. . . . [We waited to] know whether you would remain with us, whether your injuries would sap your energy, whether you would be as you had always been. We needed you so much. And today, too, M. Blum, we still need your sympathy, your understanding, your kindness, your intelligence, and your authority. . . . "There is no supreme savior . . ." . . . but these days, in the chaos of our times . . . our selfishness compels us to ask: "You, who have already given so much, please continue to help us, to enlighten us. Though we never have enough sincere and courageous leaders and representatives, we know that you are both in the highest degree, perhaps not alone but certainly above all the others."[9]

Letter after letter stressed Blum's "courage," "authority," "energy," "firmness," and "nobility." The writers admired how, "as a man," he resolutely put his values into practice. Even his political enemies recognized his determination. *Le Petit Bleu*, a conservative newspaper, asked

whether he who sows the wind is entitled to be surprised when he reaps the whirlwind. M. Blum is not a gentle prophet who preaches "Love thy neighbor." . . . And then, too, M. Blum is not dead. He was not even in danger of dying. What happened to him was a disagreeable accident but surely the least of the physical unpleasantness that a political propagandist whose doctrine is one of violence might fear. . . . The agitator's calling is not the most tranquil of careers: it brings with it the risk of attack.[10]

These words highlighted the Socialist leader's energy and will to change even as they sought to legitimate the violent reaction that such dynamic qualities provoked. The *Action Française* went so far as to justify the "tussle" by alleging that Blum had greeted the funeral procession with a raised fist, thus triggering the legitimate rage of the royalist demonstrators.[11]

Several police reports noted that "the attack on M. Léon Blum has stirred up hatred of right-wing militants and their organizations. . . . Hence we must anticipate acts of reprisal, 'punitive expeditions' against the headquarters of right-wing groups and in particular the Action Française."[12] A huge demonstration was rapidly organized to protest the attack. A police report noted that "the attack yesterday on M. Léon Blum by militants of Action Française has stirred an angry reaction in groups associated with the Popular Front. . . . A large turnout is to be expected, especially if the temperature is favorable."[13] On February 16, a large crowd marched from the Panthéon to the Place de la Nation, led by Édouard Daladier, Léon Jouhaux, Marcel Cachin, Maurice Thorez, Jacques Duclos, and Eugène Frot. More than 100,000 people sang "La Carmagnole," "La Marseillaise," and "L'Internationale." The crowd chanted "Camelots du Roi, Murderers!" "Fascist murderers!" "Soviets everywhere!" "Long live Blum!" and "Long live the Republic!" The police reported to the prefecture at five-minute intervals. At the Faculty of Law, a student provocatively made a Roman salute, with arm extended. On the Boulevard Saint-Michel, a hundred or so royalist militants, including many medical students, chanted "France for the French!" and "Soviets to the outhouse!" Some were arrested and taken to the police station on the Rue de la Huchette. On the Boulevard Saint-Germain, a young man displayed his buttocks to the jeers of the demonstrators.[14] In the eyes of the police, "so large a gathering of revolutionary forces has never before been seen in France. . . . The Communists, in particular, are rejoicing. They already see themselves on the brink of a 'legal seizure' of power demanded by the people. . . . They are absolutely certain that the next legislative elections will allow the Popular Front to score a 'smashing victory.'"[15]

For *Le Populaire*, "An entire people has risen. . . . Working-class Paris, republican Paris, the Paris of the Commune has indicated its unshakeable will to be done with fascism. . . . The odious attack on Blum was too outrageous for the people of Paris and the surrounding region not to answer the call of our Party and other proletarian parties and of all the elements of the Popular Front."[16] On the front page of *Vendredi*, Jean Guéhenno addressed an open letter to Blum: "These people hate in you what they hated in Jaurès: reason itself. They hate what we admire: your respect for the people."[17] By contrast, *L'Action Française* maintained that the demonstrators were "recently naturalized foreigners from all corners of Europe" over whom "the Jewish-alien element has little difficulty dominating." They were "fantasists who think they are helping a wealthy bourgeois like Léon Blum, a former high civil servant loaded with pensions and meddling in big business, combining the profits of statism and capitalism. . . . They represent barbarian Asia. . . . The horde does not frighten us. . . . The demonstrators, led by such leaders, are nothing but a mob of wretched serfs of Jewry and International Finance, with no chance of escaping their clutches."[18] Similarly, François Coty's reactionary nationalist newspaper *L'Ami du Peuple* also denounced the alleged Jewishness of the demonstration: "Here come the opponents of anti-Semitism: some have just emerged from the ghettos of the Fourth Arrondissement, while others come from farther away, from Poland, Russia, and Germany. . . . Next comes the delegation of the North African Star [an Algerian nationalist organization], which includes the worst of the native troops."[19]

The growing strength of the Popular Front led to electoral victory a few months later, marking a turning point in French history. With it came a revival of the most virulent anti-Semitic rhetoric. Blum's success in uniting the forces of the Left was seen by much of the nationalist and even moderate Right as a first step toward establishing a Jewish or "Asiatic" order. The tidal wave of anti-Semitic sentiment triggered by Blum's election inundated a France provoked by a sensationalist press that objected to the victory of a Jew and refused to see him as a successor of Sully, Richelieu, and Poincaré.[20] In the face of such hostility, Blum tried to discredit the many rumors that were rampant at the time, including the allegation that he was not French. In November 1938, with war looming on the horizon, he published an astonishing summary of his background for the benefit of his socialist comrades. The right-wing newspaper *Gringoire*, he said, claimed that

> the name I bear is not my own, that I was born not in France but in Bulgaria, that one of my parents was Bulgar and the other German. This myth has yet to become as firmly fixed in the public mind as that of my French châteaux, my luxurious Parisian residence, my silver dinner service, or my servants in short pants. With a little tenacity and patience, the filthy scandal sheet will no doubt take care of that. But whenever my comrades hear the rumors, this is what they should respond.
>
> I was born in Paris on April 9, 1872, a French citizen, whose parents were French citizens. My birthplace at 151 Rue Saint-Denis still exists, and any passerby can see its poor, narrow façade. . . . My father was born in the Alsatian

village of Westhoffen more than a century ago to a pair of
French citizens. My mother was born in Paris, to French
parents. My four grandparents were born French, in Alsace.
As far back as it is possible to go in the history of a family of
exceedingly modest means, my ancestors are purely French.
Ever since French Jews have had last names, my paternal
ancestors have borne the name that I bear today.[21]

The prime minister's moving evocation of his ancestors
was one of Blum's rare ripostes to the anti-Semitic madness
that enveloped him, which he normally chose to ignore. Like
Blum, the larger Jewish community believed the storm would
pass. Confident of belonging to the French nation, Jews did
not fear a return of the "anti-Semitic moment" whipped up
by the Dreyfus Affair. The front page of *La Tribune Juive* of
April 3, 1936, contained this headline: "Why We Do Not Believe in an Explosion of Anti-Jewish Hatred."[22] Prior to the
May legislative elections, *L'Univers Israélite* insisted on its "political neutrality," adding that Blum "belongs to our confession by virtue of family ties and his own statements. He has
left our community in order to lead a political party. . . . In a
few days, when he is head of government, our claims on and
duties toward him will be no greater than those of any other
spiritual family in France."[23] Similarly, *Samedi* wrote: "We are
exclusively concerned with Judaism because we are a Jewish
newspaper. We are not the ones who made M. Léon Blum the
head of the government of the French Republic. . . . We are
delighted to see that the sons of the Revolution of '89 make no
distinction among the nation's children of various persua-
sions."[24] After the results of the election were released, *L'Univers
Israélite* was pleased to see that "the predictions of the pessimists
and bad shepherds have all proved false. The campaign was not
marred by a single anti-Semitic demonstration. The age of Édouard Drumont is definitively over. . . . There are poisonous
plants that cannot grow in the free soil of France."[25] A month

later, Raymond-Raoul Lambert drove the point home: "Israel Above the Parties."[26]

These optimistic interpretations of events, which ignored the veritable flood of anti-Semitic feeling so evident in the streets and media as well as in the pronouncements of anti-Semitic groups, were not universally shared. Indeed, some prominent Jews tried to dissuade Blum from accepting the post of prime minister, a position of such prominence that it would give dangerous visibility to the Jewish community. *La Tribune Juive* wrote: "The French national socialists are wrong to think that we see Léon Blum as a gift from on high, and when we see the nastiness, vileness, hatred, and passion unleashed by the socialist leader's accession to power, we are tempted to utter a prayer normally reserved for Succoth: *Hoshana!* Save us, O Lord! Save us, our Protector!"[27] Indeed, the Consistory (the central governing body for Jewish congregations) and the Grand Rabbi of Paris apparently joined in the effort to dissuade Blum from becoming prime minister. According to André Blumel, a close associate of Blum's, "Blum was approached by the Grand Rabbi of Paris with a highly unusual offer. . . . The Grand Rabbi told him that 'if you do not accept the post of prime minister, we agree to give you a life pension equivalent in amount to the salary of the prime minister.'"[28]

For years the Grand Rabbi had been receiving letters from anxious Jews. One, René Landau, sent a copy of a letter he had written to Blum: "I am a Jew, but I am first and foremost a Frenchman in blood and heart. . . . The politics for which you are responsible has done, is doing, and will do enormous harm to your co-religionists. . . . Speaking for myself in anticipation of the day when all of your co-religionists implore you together, I ask that you give up all political activity. . . . You seem to forget that we are a minority."[29] Other Jews deeply committed to the nationalist Right, such as Edmond Bloch, and other Jewish war veterans organized an anti-Blum demonstration at the Paris synagogue, with Grand Rabbi Joseph Kaplan in attendance. The demonstrators professed not to care that Blum had been the victim of a violent attack.[30]

On the Left, by contrast, Bernard Lecache, who headed a group of Jewish organizations that supported the Popular Front, led a vigorous pro-Blum campaign, insisting that Blum "never denied his race . . . and has a singularly noble conception of the fatherland."[31] Jewish immigrant groups close to the Communist Party also supported Blum: "Jewish workers stand with the Popular Front because they oppose fascism and because they do not wish to endure the fate of their medieval ancestors."[32] The Jewish official institutions were in turmoil, so anxious about the consequence of a Jew's coming to power that the Zionist Vladimir Jabotinsky called for Jews to "evacuate" France voluntarily before they were forced to do so involuntarily.[33]

The hatred that Blum elicited was as out of the ordinary as his career, which took him from the École Normale Supérieure to the Council of State and eventually to leadership of the nation. Many French people still did not accept the republican universalism that allowed a Jew to rise to such a high position. Since the Revolution, France had been at war with itself over many issues, including the place of the Jews, and Blum's ascension brought the cauldron once more to a boil. The strong French state had given Captain Dreyfus a place on the general staff and ultimately recognized his innocence, and it was this same state that had opened the door for a Jewish civil servant to become prime minister. But the state that permitted such aberrations to occur had become alien to a part of Catholic society, which once again spewed anti-Semitic sentiments as it had done during the Revolution and the Dreyfus Affair. The latter lived in recent memory. Some who had played a leading role in it were still alive: Dreyfus himself, whom Blum, Herr, and so many others had defended, lived until 1935. On the other side, Léon Daudet, with whom Proust and Blum had rubbed shoulders during the Affair, had lost none of his anti-Semitic verve, nor had Charles Maurras and other intellectuals of the radical right.

To be sure, Édouard Drumont, the pope of anti-Semitism and the man who had almost single-handedly invented the Dreyfus Affair, was dead, but his heirs continued to speak out, and his view of the world once again seemed relevant, even if some Jewish commentators thought otherwise. His incendiary book *La France juive* (Jewish France) garnered new attention, and a host of newspapers now spread the ideas once championed by Drumont's vitriolic *Libre Parole*, which began publishing again in 1928. With Blum as prime minister, Drumont's prophecy seemed to have come true. As early as 1920, when Blum began his ascent to leadership, Daudet wrote that as Blum "talked, talked, talked . . . I could hear the prophetic laughter of Drumont, who in 1886 foresaw the arrival of a nomad of this type."[34] Hubert Bourgin, a former classmate of Blum's at the École Normale Supérieure who became an anti-Semite and supporter of the nationalist right, published an incendiary pamphlet in 1938: "His eyes flashed and darted tongues of Dantesque flame. . . . I beheld a strange and superior being in whom messianic beliefs mingled with a prophetic faith adapted to modern times, Asiatic frenzy, a European intelligence, at once French and Cartesian, and a refined aestheticism."[35]

Maurras developed an even more insulting version along similar lines, which became a leitmotif for the radical right:

> For forty years we have been describing the "career" of the wretched Carpathian, Balkan, or Rhineland Jew who arrives in the Saint-Antoine quarter in filthy rags, works in dry goods, then goes in for the stock exchange, and in the end gets shaved, cleaned up, dressed up, and even a little bilingual, adding an approximate French to his natural Yiddish. He sends his boy to the lycée and to law school and then pushes him, with a little help from all the other jewboys at the courthouse,

into the Administration and Politics, after which he runs for various offices culminating in the Chamber, the Senate, a ministry, and eventually the prime ministership. . . . That is the story of Léon Blum.[36]

In other words, the story of the man Maurras called "human detritus, to be treated as such . . . a man fit to be shot, but in the back."[37] The same story was told a thousand times using the most repulsive words and images in order to transform Blum into the quintessential symbol of "anti-France," a man to be cast out lest "the Talmud become the law of the new assembly."[38] For *Solidarité Française,* for example, "Léon Blum is a man come from who knows where, an atavism with roots in who knows what ghetto of Warsaw or Moscow, who can easily be imagined wearing the caftan of a usurer or a dog clipper, a man without a country. . . . We here are Frenchmen of France."[39] Blum the *normalien,* socialist, and art critic was thus reduced to a vulgar *Ostjuden* "in filthy rags" or the garb "of a usurer," the archetypical wandering Jew.

In a 1937 book entirely devoted to the use of Blum as an archetype of "the Jewish invasion," Maurice Bedel sang the same tune: "The prime minister belongs to a wandering race that landed by chance in Île-de-France but might equally well have ended up in New York, Cairo, or Vilna . . . and is embarrassed to be the leader of a people alien to his flesh."[40] Marcel Jouhandeau could not hide his disgust: "Although I feel no sympathy for M. Hitler, M. Blum fills me with a far deeper repugnance. . . . M. Blum is master in my homeland, and no European will ever know what an Asiatic is thinking."[41] In his eyes, "the land of Chanaan [*sic*] is today our land."[42] The celebrated historian Pierre Gaxotte protested that "the man of the soil [has been] sacrificed to the nomad and the Frenchman to the émigré," adding that "the Palestinian mare . . . hates us. He holds it against us that our sky is blue. He holds it against our peasants that they walk in wooden shoes on French soil and have no ancestors who were camel drivers wandering in the Syrian desert [with his] pals from Palestine."[43] Invoking Drumont's slogan of "France for the French," often heard during the Dreyfus Affair, anti-Semites claimed that Blum's roots were in Palestine rather than in the soil of rural France. Political figures as important as Joseph Caillaux said that Blum, unlike Jaurès, did not have "enough French soil on the soles of his shoes." The journalist Henri Béraud harped on the same theme: "Yes, indeed! My dear Léon, this is indeed an old country of fine land where it is indeed true that Grandfather Blum got no calluses on his hands from pushing a plow."[44] He went on: "There he is on the podium, nervous and pale, with the soft—too soft—eyes of an oriental wizard."[45] Maurice Bedel embroidered on the theme of French soil rejecting the foreign intruder:

> Just then, someone pointed out to M. Blum an isolated farm . . . where he would be able to converse with some of the local farmers. . . . As he stepped over a puddle of water, he lost his balance and fell. . . . I couldn't believe that [a French field] could cause a prime minister to fall. . . . It is a curious thing about the leader of the Workers' International that he seems to be afraid of contact with the soil. He doesn't wear sturdy boots for walking on country roads. . . . His nostrils have never quivered at the scent of a furrow freshly opened by the blade of a plow. He knows nothing of sap, humus, hedgerows, or stinging nettles . . . puddles after storms, mud, clay, rich soil, or good neighbors. Ah! He's not one of us.[46]

Similarly, Charles Maurras accused Blum of belonging to *le pays légal* rather than *le pays réel* (that is, the urban world of lawyers and legalities rather than the "real" France of the provinces). This accounts for the widespread myth that Blum "hated" his adversaries on the right. It is true that, speaking in the Chamber in November 1924, he said that his party "truly hates you, you and your politics," but he immediately expressed regret for this clumsy formulation. For years afterward, however, these careless words became the target of any number of hypocritical but passionate attacks by people allegedly seeking to rid France of "this foreigner who hates us."

A natural question, then, is how Blum managed to win election in Aude, in the heart of French wine country. If Blum's critics were right, such a region would hardly have wanted to be represented by a Jew who (allegedly) came from Palestine and had no roots in French soil. To make matters worse, Blum openly preferred water to wine, though he rarely turned down a good vintage. During the campaign he was subjected to vicious verbal attacks in Narbonne: he was nevertheless elected by his fellow citizens loyal to the republican ideas. Émile Sabatier, Blum's opponent in the legislative elections in the summer of 1936, asked whether "the city of Narbonne is still in France? Red Narbonne has become a transplanted corner of Palestine, in which the moneychangers have once again invaded the temple. . . . Citizens of Narbonne, how can you bear the tyranny of this man of another race?"[47] Early in 1936, *L'Indépendant de l'Aude* went Sabatier one better: "When will the yid finally decide to relinquish the Narbonne seat to a native son?"[48] The leading spokesmen of the nationalist right sang the same tune. For Maurras, Jewish gold threatened to turn Aude into Palestine.[49] The rightist newspaper *Je Suis Partout* ironically challenged Blum to drink the local wine: "Here, drink! Tell me what you think of our local plonk. Did you make a face? You despise the wine of the people who vote for you!"[50]

To be sure, the myth of "Jewish money" still influenced many propagandists, who filled their screeds with tirades against the reign of Jewish finance. Such attacks came not only from the nationalist right but also from the Communist extreme left, which denounced Blum as "an intimate of the richest cosmopolitan financiers." Maurice Thorez, the head of the French Communist Party (PCF), lashed out at "the vile lackey of City bankers," alleging that "the Socialist leader comes from the wealthy business bourgeoisie. The offices of the House of Blum are located in the heart of the Sentier, the business district, the modern temple of the Golden Calf."[51] Later, *The Soviet Encyclopedia* labeled Blum a bourgeois "closely linked to monopoly capital . . . defending fascists . . . an enemy of peace, democracy, and socialism. . . . The working class must pillory this monster."[52]

What provoked the furor of the conservative and nationalist right even more than Blum's supposed wealth or the "silver dinnerware" he was said to own was the idea that a Jew might head the government and shape the destiny of France. His presence at the head of what was still a largely Catholic and peasant nation was shocking because it contrasted so sharply with the image of the land of Joan of Arc. To be sure, the major newspapers did not refer to Blum's Jewishness, while *Le Rire* wrote: "Little does it matter that Léon Blum is a Jew and Vincent Auriol is not. One or the other will be the next prime minister."[53] Other papers approached the subject with humor: "What have I forgotten? Oh, yes: it seems that he's Jewish! . . . And you know that a left-wing Jew inevitably remains a Jew, whereas a right-wing Jew is immediately promoted to the rank of Israélite or even anointed a good Frenchman. Thus there is a whole hierarchy of gradations of treason and cowardice."[54] As during the Dreyfus Affair, when many propagandists demanded that Jews be expelled from political and administrative bodies where they would inevitably betray the national interest, now it was the Popular Front that symbolized "the Jewish Republic of France." Thousands of tracts were handed out denouncing the Jews' seizure of power by means of Blum's election as prime minister. Lists of names were circulated designating Jews employed in ministries and other departments of government—a form of public vilification. Humorists also got into the act, writing (in rhyme in the original French):

> In every ministry
> offices are chockablock
> with the pals
> of the Popular Front. . . .
> There is a whole host
> of Abramowitzes and Blochs,
> ten or more Lévys,
> and two dozen Dreyfuses.
> They're all Bretons, people say,
> of the tribe of Solomon. . . .
> In the Council of Ministers,
> when Léon Blum makes a speech,
> the interpreter records
> his speech in Yiddish. . . .
> In this strange cabinet
> there is not one Dupont or Durand.[55]

Joseph Santo, another extreme-right pamphleteer, wrote:

> Listen and exult: a Jew has succeeded Charlemagne, Saint
> Louis, Louis XIV, and Napoleon. A Jew who can say to this
> stupid, proud nation either that it wanted him or else that
> we Jews, being more intelligent, have totally outwitted you
> French. The dawn of your universal triumph is reflected in
> the jewel of Europe and the world.[56]

For Laurent Viguier, "the evil is the Jew, the Jew in public affairs. Thanks to Léon Blum, we understand this."[57] In *L'Action Française* for June 5, 1936, Charles Maurras denounced "France under the Jew." Henri Béraud wrote: "Léon Blum's distant cousins will turn up as . . . prefects, treasurers, governors, directors, etc. Next year in Parisalem, students of the Grandes Écoles will study to become leather goods salesmen. . . . And all will take heart as they read by the light of the seven-branch candelabra the complete official list of winners of the May 6 lottery."[58] According to Gustave Téry, "all the ghetto bootblacks, all the pedantic scribblers of Israel, all the wailing-walk strollers, all the rug merchants, peanut vendors, and street hawkers are in the square. The temple tailors have moved with their shears into the halls of the Republic and are ready to dispense Legions of Honor by the yard!"[59] Like the New Deal in the United States, which was referred to as "the Jew Deal" by spokesmen of the populist right who portrayed Franklin D. Roosevelt as a Jew of Dutch ancestry who would appoint Jews to his administration and undermine the Christian character of the American nation, the Popular Front revived the myth of the "Jewish Republic."[60] As in the Weimar Republic and the United States, the accession of certain Jews to political power provoked a vast wave of anti-Semitism. Just four years later, the Vichy regime would ride this wave, holding Jews in general and Blum in particular responsible for France's defeat. As at the time of the Dreyfus Affair, the charge of treason was in the air: the Popular Front was denounced by its enemies for deliberately sabotaging the state and destabilizing its institutions.

7

Popular Front!

AFTER THE Stavisky scandal, the situation evolved quickly. The right-wing riot of February 6, 1934, came as a seismic shock, which provoked the forces of the left to unite in response. On July 14, 1935, the united left staged a vast demonstration, led by Léon Blum, Maurice Thorez, Édouard Daladier, and the leaders of two rival trade union factions, Benoît Frachon and Léon Jouhaux. Finally, the attack on Blum in February 1936 and a vast movement of protest against the growing power of nationalist, xenophobic, and anti-Semitic groups accelerated progress toward unified action by the parties of the left. The attitude of the Communist Party was influenced by growing international threats, including the remilitarization of the Rhineland and the conquest of Ethiopia by Mussolini's Italian fascists. The Great Depression continued to wreak havoc: unemployment soared, the standard of living of the masses fell sharply, and growing misery brought hunger marchers into the streets. Bankrupt firms closed one after another, and anxiety deepened. On May 3, 1936, the united left triumphed in the second round of the legislative elections. The long-dominant Radical Party was reduced to just 106 seats; the Communist Party won 72 seats, a sign of its rapid progress; and the Socialists emerged as the leading party of the left with 147 seats. Despite continuing portrayals of Blum as an effeminate dandy, he forthrightly accepted his new post as prime minister on May 10.[1]

> A battle like this one requires a leader. Someone must assume full command under your permanent control. . . . When a man faces new circumstances, he must discover a new man within himself. . . . I do not know if I have what it takes to lead in such a difficult battle. . . . You will test me, and I will test myself. But one thing you will never find wanting is resolution, courage, and loyalty. . . . I do not come before you to say, "Take this chalice away, I never wanted it, I never asked for it." Yes, yes, I did ask for it, because it represents the victory of our party in a context of republican victory.[2]

The gauntlet was thrown down. The left-wing coalition of the Socialist and Radical Parties with the "loyal support" (but not the participation) of the Communist Party had found itself a "leader" in the person of Léon Blum.[3] His mission was to bring about the profound social changes his party desired while respecting the laws of the Republic.[4] Because the coalition proved to be highly disciplined, it was able to overcome the instability that had traditionally bedeviled the parliaments of the Third Republic, thus giving considerable power to the executive, as Blum desired. In this context, the powerful Communist Party turned out to be a valuable ally. It took a legalistic position: the communists insisted on maintaining order, disciplined any group that threatened to step over the line, and cautioned the rank and file that it was a mistake to think that "everything is possible."[5] The party believed it was important to avoid actions that might provoke a fascist reaction and thus threaten Soviet power.

Blum implemented ideas he had set forth in his book *La réforme gouvernementale*, published in 1936. He chose to govern with a small cabinet led by his friend André Blumel. He named Jules Moch secretary-general of the government, and Moch chose a staff of technical experts, many of whom were graduates of the École Polytechnique and capable of reacting quickly to events. Another innovation was to group several ministries together. New sub-secretariats were created, and, in keeping with what Blum had written in *Du mariage*, three of these new departments were entrusted for the first time to women—even though women did not yet have the right to vote in France. Blum even managed to persuade Irène Joliot-Curie to join the government, despite her initial refusal. "I need you," he wrote. "Above all you need *to be here*, because your mere presence will be meaningful."[6] All these steps were intended to unite the nation and respond to the emergency. Blum immediately sought to pass a series of framework laws that would set a reform agenda for the new government.[7]

The left's assumption of power in tense times kindled boundless hopes. June 1936 marked a historic break with the past, a seismic shift comparable in magnitude to the Bolshevik Revolution. Reform without revolution: that was the symbolic significance of the Popular Front. For millions of people, Blum embodied this messianic moment. Huge numbers of people invested their hopes for a better future in him. Expectations of sweeping social change were high. The masses believed utopia was within reach, and people mobilized throughout France. Strikes spread like wildfire. Many began as spontaneous walkouts but were soon taken in hand by the unions. More than two million workers participated—a sign of strong resistance to employer efforts to rationalize production, impose paternalistic management, and pay miserable wages. More than 70 percent of these strikes resulted in occupation of the workplace. Workers seized control of the machinery of production and in some cases sequestered employers. The strikes not only challenged the authority of bosses but also expressed a new sense of dignity and joy among workers. Strikes turned into celebrations, with dancing, singing, and carnivals. The number and radicalism of these work stoppages frightened factory owners. People in "the better neighborhoods" quaked in their boots. The strikes spread to the most remote corners of France; rural workers took an active part. On June 6, Blum spoke on the radio: "Any panic, any confusion, will serve the designs of the enemies of the Popular Front, some of whom are already plotting their revenge. . . . The government calls upon the country to remain calm. . . . [Our] tranquil strength guarantees further victories." Confident that the working class would behave maturely, Blum decided not to intervene to end the strikes. He supported the popular protests against injustice, and far from "betraying" the masses, as some later accused him of doing, he "interpreted" their aspirations.[8]

Things now moved quickly. Employers agreed to bargain. On June 7, following a brief government-sponsored meeting between employers and the Confédération Générale du Travail (CGT) trade union, the Matignon Accords were signed. As Blum intended, the state thus intervened decisively in labor-management relations to carve out new workers' rights, just as in the United States under the New Deal.[9] Parliament quickly passed the laws proposed by the government with overwhelming majorities. The result was a durable transformation of labor relations: firms were obliged to bargain with union locals, sanctions against strikers were prohibited, average wages were increased by nearly 20 percent, unemployment insurance was instituted, steps were taken to increase the purchasing power of workers, collective bargaining was institutionalized, the work week was set at forty hours, and workers were granted two weeks' paid vacation every year. Other key measures soon followed, including a law limiting price increases, another law changing the status of the Banque de France, and a law that socialized the crucial wheat sector and limited speculation through the Office National Interprofessionnel du Blé (National Office for Wheat Producers).[10]

Strikes nevertheless resumed throughout the country, stirring new fears, including within the government, which worried about the dangers of disorder and the possibility that violent nationalist groups might attack the factories. The Croix de Feu movement, for instance, before being outlawed and transforming itself into the French Social Party, mobilized hundreds of thousands of determined activists. On June 28, Jacques Doriot created the French Popular Party, a fascist organization, while Henri Dorgères and his Green Shirts stirred up trouble among farmers. The government committed itself to maintaining order, and Maurice Thorez, the secretary-general of the Communist Party, made a statement that remains celebrated today: "It is important to know how to end a strike when satisfaction has been obtained." Bastille Day on July 14 restored a sense of national unity: addressing a crowd of a million people, Blum celebrated the emancipatory tradition of the French Revolution, as ever a source of inspiration for him.

The mobilization of workers and farmers diminished rapidly as summer approached and people set out to enjoy their first paid vacations—for many a dream at last come true. Workers discovered the joys of camping, the sea, and the countryside. Some took up bicycling, gymnastics, and other sports, while others enjoyed the pleasures of doing nothing, relaxing with family and friends, and visiting youth hostels. Liberated from the factory for the first time, the working class discovered nature and invented a new culture of leisure.[11] Collective action restored the worker's dignity. As the philosopher Simone Weil put it, "the worker bowed his head beneath the yoke. Once the yoke was removed, he raised his head up. . . . After months and years of submission, of enduring and accepting everything in silence, he dared at last to stand up straight. To stand tall."[12] Addressing the employers' delegation at the negotiations leading to the Matignon Accords, Julien Racamond, a communist leader of the CGT, said, "Understand one thing: until today it's as though they had been in their graves. Now they have lifted up the tombstone and discovered the light!"[13] This feeling of emancipation resulted in a veritable explosion of culture: it was a highly creative moment in both film and theater as the masses became a subject for the arts.[14]

Blum—a man whom the idea of justice had inspired since childhood—made no secret of his pride in the achievements of the Popular Front. When he and other Popular Front ministers were later hauled before a court to answer charges brought by the collaborationist Vichy regime, in 1942, he said:

> I did not leave my office at the ministry very often, but whenever I did get out, I would go to the Paris suburbs and see the roads filled with old cars, motorcycles, and tandem bicycles ridden by working-class couples with matching sweaters, which showed that the idea of leisure made them think about their appearance in a natural and simple way. All this made me think that by combining work with leisure, I had in spite of everything brightened a few dark and difficult lives. We hadn't just pulled them out of the taverns or made family life easier. We had broadened their horizons and given them a kind of hope.[15]

In the wake of the vacation law especially, countless postcards addressed to Blum arrived at the office of the prime minister in the Hôtel Matignon, at Socialist Party headquarters, or at Blum's private residence on the Quai Bourbon. Some of these cards pictured forests, others the beaches of the Atlantic, the Channel, or the Mediterranean. There were photographs of sand beaches, umbrellas, and pleasure boats, or occasionally even a modest hotel such as Au Bon Vivant in Argelès sur Mer. All spoke of the joy of the paid vacation and the gratitude of the working class, expressed in the humblest, most affectionate of terms. Some of the messages are quite moving: "Dear Prime Minister and Comrade, Some comrades on paid vacation in our beautiful Roussillon have asked me to convey to you their respectful gratitude." Or this: "To Citizen Léon Blum, Long live vacations and Monsieur Léon Blum. A grateful worker." Or this one from the beach at Douarnenez: "We'll win in the end. Courage, and let's wait for the politics to play out. Vacation is a fine thing no matter what else is happening." One read, "Thanks for the paid vacation. A group of workers," and another was signed, "Comrades from the Renault factories and Galerie Lafayette."[16] There were also longer letters:

> Thanks to you, Mr. Prime Minister, workers have been able to have fun with their children on vacation. Thanks to you, Father Christmas will visit even the poorest of our comrades. For all this family happiness, Mr. Prime Minister, rejoice. . . . I salute you as the father of your country. A woman.

And this one:

> Dear Sir: I am 17 and just back from a nice trip I never would have taken but for you. . . . How can I tell how novel it felt to feel free and not to hear the factory bell or the whir of the machine, not to see certain grumpy faces, to breathe deeply and shout my pleasure from the rooftops. It was good, Sir, and I will never forget it. My father told me it was thanks to you and the Popular Front that I had a paid vacation. I therefore want to thank you.[17]

Blum was also aware of the difficulties faced by foreigners, refugees, and people working illegally in the country. Many refugees had entered France after dictatorships came to power in Germany, Italy, and Eastern Europe. Nearly three million foreigners were living in France in 1936, proportionally the highest foreign population anywhere, and many of these people had no papers and lived in extremely vulnerable situations, surrounded by virulent xenophobia and anti-Semitism. The *jus soli*, by which anyone born on French soil was automatically French, even if they had foreign parents, was challenged. After 1934, new laws were passed that restricted the right of asylum, and like most other states, France did not hesitate to shut its doors.[18] The United States, for one, established strict immigration quotas to reduce the foreign presence on American soil. In France, repression was harsh and expulsions were common. The police mercilessly pursued undocumented aliens, and the bureaucracy showed them no pity. Immigrants faced widespread hostility in a period of soaring unemployment. Although France at this point was still republican, Jewish refugees in particular found themselves in a situation of "uneasy asylum."[19] Students loudly protested their presence, while doctors and lawyers violently objected to competition from professionals among the Jewish refugees. The nationalist press denounced "the invasion of foreigners," which it blamed for the "degeneration" and "decadence" of Christian France and for creating "nations within the nation."[20]

Despite this widespread hostility, Blum courageously sought to defend the rights of foreigners. In 1935 he addressed the Chamber of Deputies: "Will you erect a wall of money between two categories of political refugee: those who can live without working and those who can live only if they work? . . . I demand that they be granted full rights of asylum, including the right to work."[21] In the same year he protested to the minister of the interior:

> Your sentiments in regard to political refugees are the noble ones you recently expressed. I think it is fair to say that these

are not the sentiments reflected in the actions of the chiefs of police and their departments at the present time. . . . In practice, the decision has been to repress as much as possible and by all available means, including raids. That is how the police usually proceed against any foreigner who falls into their hands. . . . The police today are using intolerable brutality, and policemen in the field have demonstrated unprecedented inhumanity. . . . Such methods, Mr. Interior Minister, are not in keeping with French or republican tradition.[22]

Later, in November 1938, Blum dealt with Jewish refugees from Nazism in a speech to the International League Against Anti-Semitism.

I am going to talk about the Jewish question, the tragic Jewish question, yet I am Jewish. I am a Jew who has never boasted of his background but who has never been ashamed of it either, a Jew who has always owned up to his name.

And why, after all, would I hesitate? Why would I force myself, why would I require myself to deliberately reject my past?

For many years now, I do not think anyone can say that I ever once hesitated to defend the natives of the colonies of Asia and Africa when they were oppressed by brutal officials or greedy bosses. Why, then, should I not speak out tonight on behalf of the Jews, as I have so often spoken out in the past on behalf of the Vietnamese or the Negroes of the Congo?

In a major European country, in several European countries, hundreds of thousands of Jews are today condemned to a bitter and unfortunate fate. Will they be allowed out of prison, even after being stripped of everything they own? . . . For those who have already been released or who will be released in the future, an asylum must be found. . . . Your house may already be full. That may be. But when they knock at your door, you will open it, and you will not ask them for their birth certificates or criminal records or vaccination certificates.

To be sure, these unfortunate people cannot stay forever. That is understood. It will of course be necessary to find stable, durable solutions, but for now, until they can find safer, more permanent homes, how can you refuse them shelter for a night?[23]

In the spirit of Ernest Renan, Blum favored an open, assimilationist idea of the nation and was hostile to any ethnically based notion that would exclude the Other. He embraced the universalist spirit of the French Revolution and the Dreyfus Affair. The League of Human Rights and the Citizen was created in 1898. Blum was one of the first to join, along with others who would become his close collaborators in the Popular Front, including Marius Moutet, Salomon Grumbach, Victor Basch (who became the first Jewish president of the League in 1926), and Émile Kahn (who became its secretary-general in 1932).[24] Thus members of the League who defended the rights of undocumented foreigners were keenly aware of the Dreyfus Affair. Victor Basch, who had played an important role in the Affair and who was personally close to Blum, would eventually be assassinated by the Vichy Militia. He fought valiantly on behalf of foreign refugees, because in his mind "today's fascists are the Boulangists and anti-Dreyfusards of yesteryear." Like Blum and many other League members who took part in the fight for justice under the Popular Front, Basch made no secret of his Jewishness.[25] All favored an assimilationist policy in keeping with the republican ideal of equal rights for all citizens. They sought to extend the emancipatory legislation of the Popular Front to foreigners, who gained the right to vote in professional elections and to enter various professions including public service (for those who became naturalized French citizens). Humane treatment of immigrants thus replaced the openly hostile attitude that preceded the Popular Front, even

if, in this difficult context, Blum, as a concession to the nationalists, did not favor the permanent settling of most refugees.[26]

While in power, Blum received many personal letters from
desperate immigrants begging "Comrade Léon Blum" or "Citizen Blum" to intervene on their behalf to quash expulsion
proceedings against them. One wrote from prison: "Here in
Fresnes, it is terrible to witness the barbarity of French injustice. France claims to be a land of asylum but has turned its
back on those invoking the right to asylum." A person who had
served in the French army in World War I wrote to denounce
the quota on admitting German Jews "facing either a quick
death or a slow one after a thousand tortures. . . . I know what
Jaurès would have done . . . led a vast intellectual movement
as at the time of the Dreyfus Affair. Today it is not just one
man who has been made a martyr. Thousands of us are expiat-
ing the accident of our birth in the harshest of circumstances
and, while awaiting death, cry out for help."[27] An Italian exile
wrote: "All of us exiles have confidence in you and firmly hope
that you will take steps to ensure that the right of asylum is respected." Another writer hoped Blum would help "prevent an
outrageous injustice," the expulsion of a worker named Abram
Fajnstein. In response to an urgent letter from a Greek refugee
named Antoine Papaïannou, Blum asked for the number of his
work permit and added in his own hand that "as soon as I have
this information, I will contact the Ministry of Labor." Blum
took the time to read many of these letters and often asked for
additional information so he could intervene with the bureaucracy or press a prefect for quick results.

Still, many lesser officials treated foreigners harshly. The
lower levels of the bureaucracy seemed to share the xenophobic sentiments of the larger society and resented the endless
lines of people "who don't even speak French."[28] Their cases
were dismissed without even being examined.[29] Thus it is fair
to say that "Vichy preceded Vichy," in the sense that the bu-

reaucracy of the republican state seems to have been contaminated by the ambient xenophobia to an even greater extent than during the Dreyfus Affair, and to have been influenced by the anti-immigrant propaganda spread by numerous extreme right-wing nationalist organizations.[30]

The Popular Front experiment ended all too soon. The hopes that had been raised were quickly dashed. The signs were clear as early as July 18, 1936, when Francisco Franco rebelled against the young Spanish Republic and its own popular front. On July 20, André Blumel, Blum's chief of staff, received a request for military assistance from the Spanish government. Blum immediately agreed to send bombers and artillery, but the British, whom Blum regarded as crucial allies, stubbornly refused. They were keen to preserve peace in Europe and to defend their economic interests in Spain. Meanwhile, several Radical ministers and even a few Socialists made no secret of their opposition to aid for Spain.[31] In these tense circumstances, the nationalist right launched a campaign against "Blum the warmonger" and vehemently attacked the limited military assistance offered to the Spanish Republicans. On July 25, the government announced that it would not export military matériel to Spain. Tormented and depressed, Blum thought of resigning.[32] He decided not to only after the Spanish Republicans explicitly asked him to stay.

In a speech at Luna Park on September 6, a distressed Blum addressed a crowd of Socialist militants eager to intervene in Spain: "Do you think I do not share or approve of a single thing you are feeling?"[33] He nevertheless defended nonintervention on grounds of respect for international alliances and internal differences in the government. Unofficially, Blum facilitated the transfer of arms to Spain and did nothing to prevent volunteers from joining the International Brigades. Several of his close collaborators, including Jean Zay, Pierre Cot, and Vincent Auriol, along with many Spanish leaders, regretted his pusillanimous attitude. His inaction has long been held against him and still is today. Some regard him as a "delicate soul" who betrayed the revolution.[34] By contrast, Juan Negrin, the president of the Spanish Republic who later became head of the government in exile, expressed deep gratitude to Blum in 1948: "I have learned of the disgusting political attacks on you. . . . Consider this letter as an expression of my solidarity with you. . . . No one was in a better position than I to know how concerned you were during our war and how much the republicans of Spain owe you."[35] A little later, Félix Gordon Ordas, who would lead the Spanish Republic in exile after 1951, set the record straight:

> My government feels it essential to state how much we Spanish Republicans admire in the great and humane universal personality of Léon Blum, to which we add our enthusiastic sympathy for the great French democrat and socialist, who, with such profound and humane emotion, found it in himself to commiserate with the tragedy of our war and exile. . . . We are familiar with the tragedy of Léon Blum, the politician, socialist, and Frenchman, who always had a clear understanding of the Spanish question and always sought to act justly and effectively. But he was unable to convince other democratic governments to see things as he did or to act on behalf of Spanish interests as well as justice and freedom.[36]

The trauma of nonintervention would soon come to haunt the Popular Front and arouse considerable dissent. As international tensions intensified, strikes and factory occupations resumed, while capital flight accelerated, production fell, prices rose, and unemployment increased, affecting not only the working class but also the middle class, the traditional base of support of the Radical Party, the Socialists' only ally in government. Employers renewed their all-out assault on the Matignon Accords. To make matters worse, the nationalist right went on the offensive: it launched a slander campaign against interior minister Roger Salengro, a close associate of Blum's, who was accused of deserting during World War I. Although a court-martial found him innocent, the unrelenting attacks on his honor drove Salengro to suicide on November 17, 1936. In a poignant letter to Blum, he wrote, "I am neither a deserter nor a traitor. My party has been my life and my joy. Remember me to our friends. My gratitude to you."[37] A deeply shaken Blum delivered a moving speech at Salengro's funeral. Plots fomented by extreme right groups such as La Cagoule became more and more worrisome. In response to the worsening economic situation, Blum decided to devalue the franc, but critics thought he should have devalued it even more. Rising prices ate away at the benefits of higher wages for the working class, while many commentators argued that measures intended to increase the standard of living had decreased production, already hindered by an overly rigid application of the forty-hour week.

Meanwhile, Germany had begun to rearm. Blum, an incorrigible optimist who believed that the working class was fundamentally opposed to war, had stuck with his pacifist ideals for too long.[38] At last, in conjunction with the Communist Party, which favored modernization of the army, he decided to increase the military budget significantly.[39] The consequences were immediate. By February 1937, a "pause" in Popular Front measures became necessary, throwing cold water on the hopes of the masses. Confidence in the franc collapsed, and capital fled abroad. The government was forced to put several major projects on hold and to abandon planned social reforms.

As difficulties mounted and unemployment rose, tensions with the Communists increased. Several serious incidents added to Blum's woes. In March 1937, the government refused to ban a meeting of Colonel François de La Rocque's French Social Party in Clichy. A large crowd of left-wing demonstrators turned out in protest. The police fired on the protesters, killing six and wounding more than two hundred, including a number of Communists. The Communist Party denounced the police and launched a furious attack on "the murderer Blum." Deeply depressed by the incident, Blum threatened to resign. The positions of the Socialists and the Communists on the Spanish Civil War diverged more than ever, especially after the Soviet Union agreed to send substantial military aid to the republican government to offset the extensive support in men and matériel that Italy and Germany were supplying to Franco's side. French Communist leaders, who favored aid to republican Spain, openly questioned the wisdom of supporting the Socialist government and attacked Blum with slogans calling for "cannons and planes for Spain." Blum, torn between his hostility to Franco and his judgment that the national interest required him to do everything possible to maintain the alliance with Britain, stood by his policy of nonintervention. Although the Communists continued to support the government in the Chamber, their personal attacks on Blum once again turned nasty. As Annie Kriegel wrote, "You could forget that Jaurès was a professor of philosophy. Blum was every inch the State Councilor. Thorez, though a miner, had a keener sense of fine prose than most of his peers and chose to accentuate the difference [between the two Socialist leaders] by mocking [Blum's] language, which was obviously more Stendhalian than Stalinian."[40]

The final blow came from the Radical Party, which refused to grant Blum the sweeping powers he demanded to deal with the economic crisis and flight of capital. On June 22, 1937, in the face of opposition from Radical senators who had been unenthusiastic about the Popular Front experiment from the beginning, he resigned. What happened next is quickly told: a government led by the Radical Camille Chautemps took power with the backing of the Socialists. Blum became deputy prime minister. But on January 15, 1938, Chautemps, unable to cope with numerous strikes, a deepening economic crisis, and continued capital flight, also resigned after refusing to meet the Communists' demand for higher wages. The Socialists refused to give their confidence to a government that seemed to repudiate the Popular Front coalition. After several more episodes that need not be recounted here, Blum temporarily resumed power in March. He tried to rebuild a government of national union that included the right. After failing in this, he turned to his regular allies, the Radicals, to form a new government. He proposed a Keynesian economic policy similar to Roosevelt's, including a proposal to increase the length of the work week. With international tensions on the rise, he again insisted that he be granted sweeping power to accelerate the country's rearmament. In April 1938, the parliament refused to go along with this request, and Blum once again threw in the towel.

On November 12, France swung sharply to the right behind Paul Reynaud. The forty-hour week—"the week with two Sundays"—was thrown out, as were several other concessions to the working class, while price controls were loosened, allowing inflation to resume. Wildcat strikes broke out and were harshly repressed by the police. The general strike of November 30 ended in failure, triggering a wave of government and employer repression. In December 1938, Édouard Daladier became prime minister. He broke with the Communist Party and turned to the parties of the right, marking the end of the Popular Front. Unemployment increased, industrial output stagnated, and inflation rose sharply. Violence was so ubiquitous that, as Romain Rolland noted, "an anxious Blum is right to warn the Daladier government of the danger that the bloody days of 1848 might be upon us once again, since nothing can now bridge the gap between the Republic and the people."[41] In September 1939, in a climate in which anti-Semitism was openly expressed, Blum received the following letter from a Jewish lawyer:

I attended Daladier's rally at the Arc de Triomphe. Militants from the French Social Party screamed . . . "Down with Blum!" "Death to the Jews!" A delegation carrying a banner bearing the words "Israélites of Strasbourg for the Unknown Soldier" was attacked. The flowers they were carrying were taken from them, and the banner was ripped to shreds. Daladier has gone over to the fascists and anti-Semites. My two sons were mobilized in Metz on September 23. I am disgusted. I went home and cried with my wife. My eldest son died in the last war at the first battle of the Marne.[42]

Blum now found himself cut out of political debate. The international situation complicated everything. In the summer of 1938, Hitler seized the Sudetenland, a part of Czechoslovakia, which was an ally of France. London favored compromise. Blum published several articles in Le Populaire protesting the dismemberment of Czechoslovakia.[43] On September 20, shortly before the Munich accord was signed (on September 29), Blum wrote: "War has probably been averted, but under such conditions that I, who have always fought for peace and who for many years have devoted my life to the cause of peace, can feel no joy. I am torn between cowardly relief and shame." On September 25, he insisted that "there is one thing we cannot ask of the Czechs as a matter of both justice and reason, and that is that they evacuate the Sudetenland . . . that they abjectly surrender." On September 26, he asked whether "a dreadful trap was not being laid for the government of Czechoslovakia." On September 29, when the Munich meeting was announced, he wrote: "The announcement of the Munich meeting has given rise to an outpouring of joy and hope. . . . An armload of wood has been thrown onto the sacred hearth just as the flames were subsiding and threatening to die out altogether." On October 1, again writing in Le Populaire, he confessed: "War has been averted. The scourge is receding. Life has returned to normal. People can go back to work or to sleep. They can enjoy the beauty of a sunny autumn day. How can I fail to understand this feeling of deliverance, since I share it?"

Despite this initial reaction, a sign of his deep pacifism and fear of war, Blum quickly came to his senses and initially refused to vote for the Munich treaty. Eventually, however, he gave in to party discipline, whereas the Communist Party maintained its opposition to the pact. Somewhat later, Blum overcame his doubts and openly confronted the pacifist faction of the party led by Paul Faure. He soon devoted himself fully to the fight against fascism. On October 5, he published articles in *Le Populaire* showing he had joined the camp of rearmament and confrontation with the Nazis. Germany, as he wrote on November 6, was trying to establish "pure states, homogeneous by virtue of race, language, and religion." On October 20 he wrote that "haste is essential" in building up the air force. To that end, on October 24, he called for a "mobilization of the nation's resources" despite dissent within the party. The German-Soviet pact of August 1939 came as a heavy blow. Terrified by this unnatural alliance between the Nazis and the Bolsheviks whom he had so frequently combated, he urged the Communist Party to disavow the agreement. He nevertheless condemned the government's treatment of Communists and the arrest of Communist deputies. Despite this, the Communist leaders Maurice Thorez and André Marty responded harshly, unabashedly employing the most shopworn of anti-Semitic clichés.

Blum now advocated a new government of national union similar to the one put in place during World War I. He devoted all his efforts to defending the nation and confronting the Nazi threat. In response, many on the right took up the slogan "Sooner Hitler than Blum!" Even some Socialist pacifists joined a new wave of anti-Semitism directed against "Blum the warmonger," the promoter of a "Jewish war." Charles Maurras charged that "the Jew Blum wants your head. Don't give it to him!" Léon Daudet remained true to form: "Frenchmen, young and old, from every class and walk of life, from every province and profession, are you prepared to avenge Israel for the persecutions inflicted by Hitler and the swastika? Will you enlist in the new crusade, launched from Jerusalem, to which you are invited by the ethnic hybrid and hermaphrodite Léon Blum?" Similarly, *La Libre Parole*, the paper founded by Drumont, recovered its former verve: "If you are reading this and you are French, are you prepared to die and to sacrifice your children for the Jew Blum's Crusade against the impious anti-Semite Hitler?" The last word belongs to *La Revue Hebdomadaire*, the newspaper of the nationalist right: "Warmonger Blum is the real master of ceremonies. Will France be Israel's soldier and Yahweh's instrument against the Gentiles?"[44]

8

From Vichy to Buchenwald

THE FALL of France and invasion by Germany left the country in disarray. When the Germans broke through, Blum was in London consulting with British allies. What he heard worried him: "I do not understand English. I confess this infirmity. What is called the gift of tongues is common among Jews. I have the opposite gift: an inability to learn any foreign language."[1] On returning to France, he found the political class in a panic owing to the rapid advance of German armor. As the government withdrew from Paris to Tours, Blum traveled by automobile to Montluçon, where his friend Marx Dormoy was mayor. Then, as the debacle continued to unfold, he threw caution to the winds and decided to return to Paris on June 11, 1940. He made his way across the forest of Fontainebleau, which he knew well from having toured it frequently by bicycle, only to find the capital deserted. The Chamber of Deputies was as "empty" as a "tomb," utterly abandoned. After one last visit to his apartment, where he stood a moment among his books and other familiar possessions, he again departed for the provinces, joining the steady stream of bicycles, automobiles laden with suitcases and mattresses, and horse-drawn wagons and carts of every description, all of which the Germans regularly strafed. Blum rejoined the government, which had meanwhile taken refuge in Bordeaux, as during World War I.

Chaos and anxiety were ubiquitous, and rumors ran wild. Proponents of an immediate armistice gained the upper hand. Paul Reynaud, who favored a continuation of the war, resigned, and President Albert Lebrun named Marshal Philippe Pétain the new head of government. Deputies such as Pierre Mendès-France, shocked by the idea of an armistice, decided to continue the fight in North Africa, which they planned to reach by taking passage on a ship named the *Massilia*. Blum himself thought of leaving but was prevented from doing so by a series of mishaps. The *Massilia* turned out to be a trap. The deputies who sailed were accused of cowardice and desertion, when in fact they had chosen to reject defeat and fight the enemy. As the new government negotiated an armistice with Germany, Blum sought refuge near Toulouse with the children of his friend Eugène Montel.

The question of his departure became urgent. Friends urged him to leave the country quickly because he was in danger not only as a Socialist but also as a Jew. On June 16, 1940, Admiral François Darlan himself ordered "French naval authorities to facilitate if need be the embarkation of [former] Prime Minister Léon Blum aboard any naval ship or aircraft headed to North Africa."[2] Meanwhile, Édouard Herriot offered urgent advice to Georges Mandel and Léon Blum: "You two should leave no matter what happens. Do not remain in the clutches of our present masters. I know how much they hate you." Blum's old comrade Vincent Auriol offered similar counsel: "They will hunt down Socialists. They will humiliate

Jews. And you are both a Socialist and a Jew, to say nothing of being you."[3] Blum refused.

> If I were to leave now, it would only be to take up my post as a civilian soldier in the battle that Great Britain today and perhaps the United States tomorrow will wage against the enemy. . . . No, you see, now that the Government has capitulated, there is for me only one party and one duty: to stay in France, where I am, calmly awaiting danger if indeed there is danger, ready to answer for my past actions in any public debate, at the podium in the Chamber if I can or at the bar in a court of justice if I must. My duty is calmly to defy the injustice and hatred that have been set loose in the land. . . . I feel that I cannot on my own, especially in this hour, break the tie of solidarity that binds me to my country. . . . I believe that France has dishonored itself, but I do not think I have the right to save myself. I must share the common fate not only in misfortune, which is relatively easy, but also in shame.[4]

Blum fought the new regime and did not hesitate to visit Vichy, the seat of Marshal Pétain's government.[5] He went there on July 4. Dumbfounded by the proposed constitutional reform granting all power to Pétain, he maintained that such a "coup was unprecedented in our history; it surpasses the 18th Brumaire and the 2nd of December [i.e., the coups of Napoleon and Napoleon III]." He tried to rally Socialist representatives in Vichy against the plan. At first, they seemed willing to go along with him, but "the venom visibly spread. . . . Within a few hours, thoughts, words, and faces had become almost unrecognizable. . . . The poison whose effects were plain to see was quite simply fear, panicky fear. . . . People were carried away by collective currents of terror and cowardice, like a frightened mob. . . . They listened with bowed heads and submitted. Most had succumbed to the poison and accepted their fate."[6]

On July 10, 1940, Blum was thunderstruck when a majority

of his Socialist comrades rallied behind the new government of Pierre Laval. Irony of ironies, the assembly that voted to grant full powers to Marshal Pétain overlapped to a large extent with the Popular Front assembly elected in 1936, minus the twenty-seven deputies who had sailed for North Africa on the *Massilia* and of course the Communist deputies who had been excluded on September 27, 1939, after the Nazi-Soviet pact was signed. Danger was everywhere, and there was reason to fear the worst: among the eighty courageous deputies who opposed Laval's new constitution granting full powers to Pétain, only thirty-six were Socialists, ninety other Socialists having chosen to join Laval. In this dramatic moment, with his own life at stake, Blum, the former leader of the party, found himself abandoned by most of his troops. "Moses became Lear," one of his later biographers wrote.[7] He slipped out a back door to avoid the insults of the mob and returned to the home of Montel's children, "L'Armurier." On August 17, the Prefecture of Haute-Garonne issued him a new identification card, which indicated that his hair and mustache were grey, his nose "straight," and his complexion "clear."[8] The madness of Vichy seemed far away. At L'Armurier, he met with collaborators and friends from the Popular Front such as Jules Moch and André Blumel, who argued against his optimism and warned him that Vichy's leaders "would promulgate their racist laws, made in Germany, and organize their own Gestapo."[9] Blum nevertheless remained confident. In broad strokes he outlined how Germany would be defeated and Britain, the United States, and the USSR would win the war. In no uncertain terms he pledged his support to General Charles de Gaulle: "During those days and weeks of patriotic incubation, it became clear that the leader of 'Free France' was not just a soldier. Only a soldier could have commanded such trust, such talent, such obedience. . . . Official France might have capitulated, but 'Free France' carried on the fight."[10]

On September 15, at six in the morning (respectful of the law against nighttime arrests), the police surrounded the house. Blum was arrested and incarcerated, along with Georges Mandel, Édouard Daladier, Paul Reynaud, and General Maurice Gamelin, in a medieval castle at Chazeron in the Massif Central. Conditions were harsh: the cells were cold and lacked running water. This was only the beginning of a long ordeal, which Blum faced simply, without complaint. The surveillance was strict:

> Surveillance must be constant and vigilant. . . . The police officer in charge and guards shall remain in the guard room, whose door shall remain open in order to maintain a close watch on the door of room number ___ . . . The guard post will remain illuminated at all times. The officer in charge shall be armed with an automatic pistol. . . . Mr. Léon Blum may leave his apartment only to go to the toilet, in which case he shall be followed by a civilian official to the door and accompanied back to his room in the same manner.[11]

Blum returned to his beloved Stendhal and devoured the works of Virginia Woolf and others that he found in the castle library.[12] In his misfortune he took comfort from the frequent visits of Renée Blum, a Protestant-born Geneva woman married to his son Robert, who was a prisoner of war in Germany. Renée became close to Janot, Blum's mistress, who was not allowed to visit the castle. Both did all they could to assist him. Blum wrote many affectionate letters to Janot: "Could you see me behind the bars? I waved my handkerchief at you."[13] He and Janot maintained their intense relationship by way of letters and notes carried back and forth by Renée. Within a few months, Janot obtained permission to visit Blum herself.

On November 16 he was transferred to the Château de Bourrassol in the Massif Central near Riom, where he was to be tried. The castle was in ruins and bitterly cold. Living conditions were even worse than in Chazeron: Blum's only toilet was a filthy chamber pot, and water froze in his room. Daladier described the scene in his diary: "Rainy, awful weather. But in the afternoon, Blum, during his exercise period, sat in the sun on a roadside marker. Basque béret, long, thin body, almost white drooping mustache. Prophet of Israel."[14] Janot was able to contact the justice minister, Joseph Barthélemy, who made no secret of his anti-Semitic feelings but granted her the right, as Blum's secretary, to visit him for the purpose of writing "a work of history."[15] Blum was also allowed to receive a few faithful friends. A living symbol of the reviled Popular Front as well as a Jew, he became the target of vicious attacks by the collaborationist press, which blamed the Jews in general and Blum in particular for France's defeat. After his friend Marx Dormoy was assassinated on July 25, 1941, Blum knew that anything could happen to him.

In a way, Vichy represented the nationalist right's revenge for the Dreyfus Affair. Only thirty-four years separated the end of the Affair from the birth of Vichy, and any number of frustrated anti-Semites from the Dreyfus years, including Charles Maurras, were still active. They had not changed one bit. They still called for Jews to be expelled from government and the public arena, as well as excluded from most professions and stripped of civil rights. All state Jews—be they deputies or senators, state councilors, judges, prefects, military officers, or teachers—were dismissed from public service. Vichy answered the prayers of the most zealous anti-Dreyfusards: the Jewish statute of October 4, 1940, one of the very first measures taken by Vichy, made the government of France *judenrein*. Blum and many of his closest friends from the Council of State, such as Paul Grunebaum-Ballin, were affected. A small number protested vehemently, insisting that their families had been French for generations, that their parents had made sacrifices in France's wars, that they themselves had been decorated in World War I and had always served France loyally. They wrote to Marshal Pétain, whom many had met in the course of their careers, asking that he intervene to prevent the Jewish statute from being applied to them and later asking him to block their deportation—all in vain.[16] Blum, certain of his rights and his legitimacy and unafraid of reprisals, refrained from protesting his arrest or requesting special treatment. He courageously defended his actions as prime minister as well as his Jewish identity, which he never tried to hide.

On October 16, 1941, after Blum had been in prison for a year, Marshal Pétain announced in a radio speech that a special Political Justice Council had decided that Blum, Daladier, Cot, and Gamelin would be transferred to a fortified installation.[17] Pétain expressed his wish that the trial would proceed quickly and concluded his speech by anticipating its outcome: "I assure you that although you were betrayed, you will not be disappointed."[18] The accused were taken to the Fort de Portalet, a castle in Urdos in the Pyrenees—a sinister mountainside fortress surrounded by barbed wire and virtually inaccessible. In his solitude, Blum wrote *À l'échelle humaine* (On the Human Scale), which begins with this memorable passage: "The lock on my door and the bars on my window have not separated me from France. . . . I feel my heart at every moment beating in unison with the heart of France."[19] Janot found a place to live nearby and resumed their correspondence. Blum wrote: "On waking I rushed to my window. My first impression was somber. The window opens directly on a vertical wall of rock. . . . I saw you on the road, I saw you speak with the guard at the sentry box and start across the bridge, but I have little hope. . . . A ray of sunshine just made its way into my room, which had seemed impossible. Is that a good sign?"[20] Janot was able to visit again, but soon thereafter, on December 30, 1941, Blum was abruptly removed from Portalet and returned to Bourrassol.

Vichy had planned a show trial to lend legitimacy to the

new regime. On October 8, the prosecutor, Gaston Cassa-gneau, handed Blum an "additional indictment" that included a lengthy critique of the Popular Front and ended with these words: "Because the unjustifiable weakness of M. Léon Blum's government compromised both production in the short run and the moral state of the producers, he betrayed the duties of his office." By failing to rearm France and tolerating a se-ries of debilitating strikes, he was responsible for the defeat. Blum, a shrewd lawyer, planned a vigorous defense against the charges. Like Dreyfus on his island, he prepared in solitude to confront a regime that had repudiated all his values. He ob-jected to the very brief time he was given to prepare his de-fense: "In short, you are inviting an already condemned man to respond to the indictment your office has prepared. What is that if not a cruel mockery of justice? . . . Hasn't the case al-ready been decided?"[21] He nevertheless prepared his defense carefully, studied the documents, and analyzed the record. A first phase of interrogation took place in November and De-cember 1941, followed by a second phase in February 1942. Blum showed that as prime minister he had prevented civil war, forestalled bloody clashes, and implemented social legislation that improved the physical condition of the working class and thus created conditions favorable to rearmament. His interro-gators did not let up, however. The Popular Front as a whole, including the forty-hour week, paid vacations for workers, and tolerance of strikes, was held responsible for the military de-feat. Blum's answer was straightforward and logical:

> When one imputes criminal responsibility to a man, a leader
> of government, without proving or even alleging any per-
> sonal fault, without articulating a single fact against his hon-
> esty, honor, or professional duty or alleging a single failure
> of effort, application, or conscience, when his only crime is
> to have implemented the policy prescribed by sovereign uni-
> versal suffrage monitored and approved by the Parliament

to which sovereignty has been delegated by the people, then one is no longer trying a man or a head of government but the republican regime and the republican principle itself.[22]

This would become the central thread of his defense. The trial began on February 20, 1942. Standing before his judges, surrounded by enemies determined to destroy him, and accompanied by his attorneys, Blum courageously began his summation of the defense case on March 10. He spoke for several hours and offered nothing less than an indictment of the Vichy regime.[23] Denouncing Vichy for putting the Republic on trial, he turned the tables on the court. In his view, it was the reactionary right and the plots hatched by La Cagoule that had provoked the masses and brought the Popular Front to power. It was the right that had aggravated the crisis and mobilized the working class, leading to factory occupations that Blum was able to limit by negotiating the Matignon Accords, putting France back to work and thus facilitating rearmament. As he saw it, social reform had not hindered production but increased it. Blum doggedly defended his policies and repeatedly interrupted the judge, corrected his pronouncements, commented ironically on the proceedings, introduced highly technical arguments about weaponry, and throughout stood his ground with aplomb. He also defended his decisions with regard to Nazi Germany as well as his social policies. To prevent war, France had not only to rearm rapidly but also to maintain a dialogue with other countries. In his widely heard summation, he admitted that he had agreed to receive Hjalmar Schacht, Hitler's representative, at Matignon:

> Had I been the man I have been portrayed as, I might have told him: "I am a Marxist. I am a Jew. I will not talk to a state in which all socialist organizations have been outlawed and Jews are persecuted." But instead I said: "I am a Marxist. I am a Jew. That is why I am so eager for this conversation

between us to produce results." . . . I had only the interests of our country in mind. At the same time, I carried out the largest rearmament plan of all time. I fulfilled the duties of my office. I fulfilled my duties as a Frenchman.[24]

Blum's confession drove *Le Petit Parisien* wild: "'I am a Marxist and I am a Jew! With the impudence of his race he made this declaration to the court. . . . His only chance of regaining power, of once again raising his Jewish and Marxist fist over France, is a Bolshevik victory. That is what he wants. That is what he is hoping for." *Le Cri du Peuple* reiterated the words of Xavier Vallat, who was present in the courtroom: "The first Jew to have governed our old Gallo-Roman country." It ran headlines such as "The Jew Dodges," "The Jew Wants It All," and "The Impudent Jew Accuses Our Marshal." *Au Pilori* did not mince words: "This accursed race has a lot of nerve." *Jeunesse* was not surprised that Blum "in his Jew skin failed to muster any energy, patriotism, or pride," while *L'Appel* attacked the "leader of the Popujew Front" and *Paris-Soir* mocked those of Blum's friends who "formed a circle around the wailing wall where Blum has been sobbing for the past few days." For *Gringoire*, finally, when Blum spoke, "he looked like an offspring of his ancestors. He represented the persistence of the Jewish idea. . . . He persisted in being what he is. A Jew! Nothing but a Jew! But a whole Jew!"[25]

Two Jewish statutes had been in force in France for more than a year. French Jews had been rounded up. Anti-Semitic persecution grew worse with each passing day. And close friends of Blum's such as Marx Dormoy had been assassinated. Yet Blum did not fear to proclaim his Jewish identity or his adherence to Marxism (which was in fact quite debatable). Facing down enemies who were after his head, he made it perfectly clear that a French citizen could also be a Jew and that a Jew could unhesitatingly fulfill "his duties as a Frenchman."

He made it clear that the pact between France and its Jews, a part of the revolutionary and republican heritage, remained in force despite the ideology of Vichy and the Nazi occupation. In a magniloquent conclusion to his summation, Blum again invoked the names of Marx and Jaurès:

> Gentlemen, I am done. You can of course condemn us. But I do not think that your judgment can undo our efforts. I do not think—this may seem boastful—that you can eliminate us from the history of this country. . . . We are not some monstrous excrescence in this country's history, because we were a government of the people. We stand in what has been this country's tradition since the French Revolution. We did not disrupt the legacy, we did not break the chain, we welded it back together and made it more secure.[26]

The chain that linked Léon Blum to the French Revolution symbolized both the dream of a liberated people and the utopia of emancipated Jews at last become citizens. It was a chain that linked all citizens regardless of social class or religious identity, establishing a solidarity based on the idea of justice.[27] It was more than Vichy's leadership could comprehend and more than the Germans could tolerate. Blum managed to cast doubt on their legitimacy. He openly questioned their authority and mocked them publicly.

The press did not conceal its anger at the audacity of Blum and Daladier, who transformed themselves from accused into accusers. *L'Action Française* proposed "a bonfire to burn the Declaration of the Rights of Man and the works of Rousseau, Kant, and Blum." *Je Suis Partout* complained that "instead of killing these bastards, we gave them a platform," while *Les Nouveaux Temps* stated flatly that "the accused at Riom should have been hanged a year and a half ago. The authorities allowed them to transform the courtroom into a branch of the Radical and Socialist conclave. Can this be tolerated?" Shocked by the sight of Blum defending himself, *Au Pilori* blasted the "Jew Léon Blum-Suss": "We want heads!" For *La Gerbe*, "Blum was still a Karfulkenstein [a name invented by anti-Semites to mean foreign Jews] whose ancestors scratched their lice in the shadow of the Carpathians." *L'Appel* made no secret of its admiration: "You are a magisterial Jew. The imbecilic Vichyites you so diabolically deceived don't come up to your cloven hoof." *Le Cri du Peuple* wrote that "for Blum and Daladier, the court became the ideal place to denigrate the Marshal's work." *Le Petit Parisien* insisted that the trial was "an immense fraud . . . a platform for agitation against the Marshal."[28] Jules Blacas addressed the working class: "French worker . . . shake off all the Blums hanging on your shoulders and sucking your blood like a tick or louse. They're not French! They stink of the ghetto and hate you."[29]

Any number of abusive letters reached Blum in his prison cell: he was called a "hypocrite and wailing manure," a "kike saboteur of the nation," and a "sinister bandit guilty of bringing France down." Marcel Déat wrote that "what I hold Léon Blum responsible for is de-virilizing French Socialism and turning it toward Talmudism. . . . Blum's central crime . . . is to have submitted to the tyranny of his race, to have passionately propelled France toward massacre."[30] He did nevertheless receive a few letters of encouragement from "French workers [who] have not forgotten what they owe him," from "shop floor comrades" in Grenoble who "extend their sympathy and encouragement," from workers in "the Renault artillery plant" who sent their "proletarian salute." Other correspondents were convinced that "history will bring justice to the accused."[31]

Unable to cope with such an unyielding defendant, Vichy threw in the towel on April 11, suddenly calling a halt to a trial that was undermining its legitimacy, especially when international correspondents covering the case expressed "admiration" for the defendant, eliciting an indignant response from the collaborationist press.[32] Blum returned to his cell at Bourrassol. The Germans were furious. Hitler personally ordered an end to the trial. Joseph Barthélemy remarked that "the Germans were shocked to see a Jew attacking a marshal. . . . In Germany, no Jew would dare to speak out against Hitler."[33]

Blum quietly returned to his work. He received letters of encouragement from Édouard Herriot, who spoke of his "loyal friendship . . . [and] unwavering devotion," Jules Moch, André Philip, Vincent Auriol, Pietro Nenni, and Roger Martin du Gard. "If the sympathy of those whose thoughts have been with you for the past twenty years can be of any comfort in this strange ordeal," Martin du Gard wrote, "my wife and I wish to be counted among them. . . . With a heavy heart and esteem that remains with you in misfortune."[34] Blum resumed his correspondence with General de Gaulle via messengers who traveled clandestinely between France and England. He assured de Gaulle that when France was liberated, "he [de Gaulle] will be the necessary man, or, rather, the only possible man when the idea of resistance and the fact of liberation form a bond among the French." Therefore, "the government can have only one leader: the man who awakened and who embodies the spirit of Resistance in France."[35] On several occasions he warned de Gaulle that if it proved necessary "to wipe the slate clean" of Vichy institutions and swiftly seize power, he should nevertheless respect the will of the people and the essential role of political parties, "since France will become a democracy again, won't it? And there is no democratic government without political parties."[36] De Gaulle did not fail to respond: "We here are aware of your admirable firmness. We are not ignorant of your struggles and trials. . . . Liberation is coming. . . . Rest assured that we know what role the Socialist Party played in the Resistance, in its front ranks." After seeking Blum's "accord and cooperation" on various projects, de Gaulle added: "I beg you, Mr. Prime Minister, to accept this assurance of my deep and devoted respect."[37] Later, de Gaulle assured Blum that he could not "imagine how a government could be established or govern" in liberated France without Blum's cooperation.[38]

Ignoring his own vulnerable position, Blum patiently worked to rebuild and reorganize the Socialist Party with the help of Daniel Mayer, who worked underground to integrate Socialist resistance networks with the National Resistance Committee.[39] Blum protested when de Gaulle seemed to favor the Communist resistance network over the Socialist one, although he was also committed to bringing the Communist Party back into French politics after the war, provided that the USSR returned to the international community and the French Communist Party rejoined the French community. Blum insisted on this because "French Communists are risking their lives. They are in the front ranks of the victims of repression as well as in the Resistance. Hitler has singled them out along with the Jews as hostages and victims."[40] From his prison cell Blum thus tirelessly carried on the fight against Vichy and its German allies.

After Allied troops landed in North Africa, the Germans reacted rapidly. On November 11, 1942, they invaded the Southern Zone and occupied all of France. From his prison, Blum could see German troops moving south. He worried not only for himself but also for Janot, who was also Jewish. He had been horrified by the roundup of Paris Jews by French police in July 1942 and was fully aware of another roundup near Riom of foreign Jews, who had been sent to the transit camp at Drancy. He wrote:

> A steady stream of German cars and trucks moved down the highway. . . . It was the first time I had seen anything like it.
>
> Janot, my love, writing to you calms me down. I should have done it sooner. . . . What I want to say at once is that I admire you. I admire your courage, your firmness, and the calm you bring to the inevitable inner turmoil, my beloved. I admire your existence. I admire your love. And when I think

of the state of nervous exhaustion, physical overwork, and chronic insomnia you must have been in when these stunning events took place. . . . Janot, my love, I hope you don't have to pay for all this.[41]

The only way he could think of protecting her was to marry her. Blum wrote to his attorney: "If she were my regular and lawful wife, she might have a little less difficulty. In my eyes, this is the decisive reason. It is the reason I have been able to overcome the private doubts I've confided to you."[42] Overtures were made to Vichy. Joseph Barthélemy, the minister of justice, was contacted once again, and he facilitated the marriage. A ceremony was arranged, but last-minute administrative difficulties intervened. Life went on. Blum learned that his only possession, a small plot of land near Narbonne, had been seized. The "property of the Jew Léon Blum" was put up for public auction.[43]

Nothing derailed him. On February 3, 1943, he wrote to a friend, one Madame Camel: "I received your package from Noch. The ham hock was wonderful. I haven't yet eaten the prunes, but I know the species and look forward to eating them. . . . The household routine remains the same, except that occasionally new guards appear from outside."[44] Suddenly, however, on March 31, 1943, things changed. After visits from René Bousquet, the secretary-general of the Vichy police and the man responsible for the July 1942 roundup of French Jews, and the no less redoubtable Colonel Helmut Knochen of the SS, representing Himmler, Blum was removed from Bourrassol by German troops. Thus began the much-feared journey into the unknown. He had just enough time to send a few last letters to Janot: "Tonight all my thoughts are with you. . . . I dare not hope I will see you again. . . . My heart is broken, but do not doubt my courage or endurance. What will become of you? . . . I think of you constantly." And this: "I have no hope of seeing you today. I think of you constantly. You are everywhere, and especially in my thoughts. . . . Know with certainty, absolute certainty, that I am holding up well and will continue to do so. . . . I worry for you. . . . I will write you every day as if certain that my letters are reaching you. My heart belongs to you." And finally: "I will momentarily be leaving this place, which has been ours. My thoughts are and will remain with you. I promise you I will return intact. I hug you. Léon."[45] *Le Populaire*, now being published clandestinely and passed "from hand to hand," protested and issued fanciful threats:

> Léon Blum deported!! He is the leader of French Socialism. He was the head of the Popular Front government. In addition —since this point has been raised by the bloody butchers from across the Rhine—he was born a Jew. All these qualities place him in grave danger. The Socialist Party, which has taken steps in response to the situation, has drawn up a list of hostages who will answer for anything that happens to him. They are Philippe Pétain, Pierre Laval, Bousquet, and Barthélemy.[46]

Taken to Germany as a valuable prize potentially useful in some future prisoner exchange, Blum was held in Buchenwald, where he was guarded by the SS. He was confined some distance away from the camp where so many deportees died, in a small hunting lodge that Himmler had built. In a cruel twist of fate, the lodge was situated on the very hill where Goethe had once liked to meditate. Blum shared quarters but not ideas with Georges Mandel, a strict proponent of law and order, a patriot and adversary of the Popular Front, and a Jew detested, as Blum was, by the extreme right, with which he nevertheless maintained cordial relations in the face of common threats. "I was in the hands of Nazis," Blum wrote. "For them I represented something more than a French politician. I also embodied what they hated most in the world, since I was a democratic socialist and a Jew."[47]

He would spend two years in Buchenwald. Less than a month after arriving, he began a correspondence with his beloved son Robert, who was a prisoner of war at Lübeck. On April 27, he confided to Robert how "wrenching" it had been to leave France. He nevertheless reassured his son that he was coping well with the change of diet and climate and passing the time by rereading Rousseau's *Confessions*, Shakespeare's plays, the works of Alfred de Musset in the Pléiade edition, Mme de Lafayette, the *Mémoires* of La Rochefoucauld, Gide's *Journal*, Goethe's plays, Cicero, and one of his favorite works by Stendhal, *Lucien Leuwen*, which he rediscovered along with Stendhal's correspondence. He also told Robert that he hoped Janot would be allowed to join him.[48] On Saturday, June 19, his hope was realized: "I want to tell you of my great joy: Janot arrived here last night. I have known for twenty-four hours she would be coming, but I couldn't believe it, and a superstitious fear kept me from telling you until she actually arrived."[49] After many consultations, a probable intervention by Laval, and approval by the Germans, Janot was allowed to join Blum.[50]

Despite the inevitable anxiety, the tragedy of the situation, the threat hanging over them, and the uncertainty of their fate, the couple settled into a quiet daily routine in the hunting lodge guarded by a detachment of thirty SS troops. Another prisoner, a Jehovah's Witness, served as Blum's aide-de-camp. Janot took care of the house and cooked while also reading Goethe, Pascal, Tolstoy, and Saint Augustine. The three prisoners— Léon, Janot, and Georges Mandel—enjoyed lively conversations, commenting on events, discussing books, and listening to Brahms, Beethoven, Bruckner, Gluck, and even Wagner's *Valkyrie*. Blum received many letters from his son, who offered reassurance about the health of family members. He took daily walks, although "the compound was quite small and the ground was often soaked by rain and mist."[51] He told his son about his health worries, his rheumatism and migraines, and complained of oppressive heat and glacial cold but also assured him that nothing serious was wrong: "Everything is in working order," even though the lodge was buried in snow.

On October 8, 1943, he and Janot were married. The couple signed a German marriage contract that had been drawn up by a Weimar notary. On December 30, 1943, they celebrated the New Year. Janot had made "Christmas trees [and] cooked an excellent soup and a savory pie as well as a tart." The summer of 1944 began quietly: "Nothing of note in our sylvan solitude."[52] He added: "We are keeping an eager eye on our vegetable garden."[53] Back in France, the marriage did not go unnoticed in certain quarters. The police took note of the event:

> The former prime minister, who is 71, married for the third time, a Jewess. In the present circumstances, this is not without significance, or at any rate Socialist militants have given it one, namely, that Blum wishes to demonstrate to other Israélites that in a period in which they are persecuted, he will not deny his race. On the contrary, he affirms it and thus demonstrates his faith in the mission of Judaism. The announcement of this marriage has given rise to considerable commentary, revived passions, and aroused a good deal of criticism from anti-Semitic members of the SFIO. . . . Many feel that the news has been publicized rather ostentatiously and all too clearly indicates the future intentions of the former leader of the SFIO, thus provoking some rather strong reactions from those who believe that Blum did more for the Jews than for socialism.[54]

The relative calm of Blum's letters may seem surprising, but of course he knew nothing of the tragic circumstances of the nearby concentration camp. In any case, the quiet was suddenly shattered after Philippe Henriot was assassinated at the end of June 1944. The Gestapo came for Blum's fellow prisoner Georges Mandel and took him back to France. Blum and

Janot helped him pack and bade him an emotional farewell. A few days later, his body was found in the forest of Fontainebleau. The murder of their friend grieved the couple deeply.[55] "Filled with sinister forebodings and thinking that sooner or later we would follow the same path," Blum believed the end was near. He quickly drafted a will and sent it to his son on July 31. Oddly enough, he gave a second copy to the camp commandant, who promised to pass it on in case of "accident." After repeating that he owned nothing other than his books and furniture, he mentioned that he had married Janot under the regime of "separation of property" and added what he considered essential, a summary of his final thoughts.

> Writing from my German prison, amid the boundless horrors inflicted on my country, my party, and my race, I repeat what I have said and written in other times and places. Not only have I not succumbed to contagious thoughts of reprisal, correction, or repression; not only do I not renounce any of my past convictions; on the contrary, I persist in them with greater certitude and more ardent faith than ever. The conditions for a true and lasting peace remain what they have always been, as do the conditions for social justice. They are not at the mercy of our national or personal misfortunes. My dearest wish is that the French people, Socialists, and Jews join the front ranks of those fighting for these goals. They should ask for nothing else and demand no other compensation for the suffering they have endured. For a *short* period after the war, it may even be possible and therefore necessary to go farther than I ever hoped in the direction of universal (and not European) organization of economic internationalism, toward political and legal supra-sovereignty. But no organization will be stable unless it takes its inspiration from a spirit of human fairness, equality, and, *as soon as possible*, trust.

Blum ended his will with a series of recommendations to his son, whom he asked to "pay his debt" to Janot's children, to show them as much kindness as he himself would have shown, because they were the children of "the person who gave me her all, without whom I would have found it difficult to bear my burden over the past four years and who has made this cruel period of my life a time of deep happiness." His letter ended with an expression of confidence in the future: "I do not bid you or anyone else farewell. I will see you again. . . . I will see everyone I love again. Everyone who remains." Then, to make sure that his ultimate beliefs were clear, he added this codicil:

> The wave of cruelty we have seen rising in one nation over the past five or ten or more years and which today is sweeping across the world exists, I am convinced, in latent form everywhere, and it doesn't take much for it to bathe the foundation of civilization in its bloody filth. I no more believe in a race of brutes or a master race than in fallen or damned races. I reject the condemnation of Germans on racial grounds as I reject it for Jews. I am cruelly aware, I swear to you, of what has happened and is happening every day. But I also remember a spring morning when I was nearly stomped to death on a sidewalk by a purely French mob. I remember the horrifying spectacle of Vichy in July '40. Re-read [Henry] Houssaye's *1815*. Everything that is now being said and written about the Germans and their collective responsibility and ethnic inevitability was said and written about the French in England and Germany after Waterloo. A small change in circumstances is enough to awaken the brute in man, in all men. . . . I am convinced that all people can respond to a treatment of reason mixed with kindness, firmness, and trust. If peace were to be concluded in a spirit different from this, the violence would merely have changed camp for a few years, and, as Jaurès used to say, nations would again begin passing the poisoned cup of the Atrides from one to another. The danger is greater in periods when everyone thinks he is a victor than when everyone feels vanquished.[56]

In a similar state of mind, opposed to determinism of any kind, Blum compared the fate of Germans and Jews. In notes he made in Buchenwald, he wrote: "An outcast people is like a persecuted people. Persecution isolates, preserves, and fixes the peculiar character of a people. The Jewish people. One nation has crucified another. I want no revenge. . . . It has to be the Jewish people that begs, in the name of its martyrdom, that nothing degrading be done to the Germans. People say they have always been like that and always will be. My response as a Frenchman, my response as a Jew, is that I do not accept a racial theory of the Germans. No race is predestined to evil."[57]

Blum also offered advice about the future of France, advice inspired by the same ideas of necessary reconciliation, in this case of French with French:

> Do not be the Chambre Introuvable of the Resistance [the reference is to the intransigent ultra-royalist parliament of 1815, which refused to accept the results of the French Revolution]. . . . You are émigrés like [Victor] Hugo, not [Louis de] Bonald. . . . Exclude the unworthy from public life and even national life but make no reprisals. Avoid all cruelty. Do nothing to hinder national reconciliation. Do not invite the revenge of pity, inevitable in France. . . . Consider the consciences of the men who in good faith mistook their duty and misconstrued the national interest. . . . Nights of August 4 [the allusion is to an episode of the French Revolution in which the aristocracy voluntarily renounced its privileges] are short summer nights, and the opportunity comes only once. That is your task. . . . I fear that a false Jacobinism may turn you away from the true revolutionary spirit.[58]

Life in Buchenwald continued despite almost daily bombing. Blum and his wife lived quietly except for various problems of health. Blum often reassured his son that he was fine, apart from a troublesome boil near his eye: "We are living an orderly life, almost monastic in its regularity, simplicity, and frugality," he wrote, adding that "our solitude, which is absolute but shared, is not oppressive."[59] On August 24, however, as he would later recount in *Le dernier mois* (The Last Month), American planes bombed the Buchenwald concentration camp, after which Blum saw for the first time prisoners "hitched like draft animals to a wagon overloaded with rocks and sand and others walking in a line bearing a long tree trunk on their stooped shoulders like captives in an Egyptian or Assyrian frieze." Although he and Janot had long been aware of "the strange odor" that entered their window at night, and although they knew that many people were dying in the camp, they did not know "how they died" and were kept entirely in the dark about the existence of crematory ovens. Only later, after the camp was liberated, did they learn of "the almost demented horror" of the place.[60]

In December 1944, Blum celebrated Janot's birthday: "I hope my letter will convey to you the depth of my love, which has only grown stronger and richer as we live together more completely and more entirely alone. . . . I love you. Léon."[61] He immersed himself in Stendhal's *The Red and the Black* and *Armance* as well as in Flaubert, Molière, Racine, and Choderlos de Laclos's *Dangerous Liaisons*. Early in 1945 his health took a sudden turn for the worse. He suffered from terrible lumbago, "an unbearable pain in the back. I felt as if I were doubled over, broken in two, like a paralytic." He sat with his "leg stretched out on a stool, like a gouty old soldier."[62]

On April 1, however, everything changed abruptly. SS troops came looking for Blum and his companion and, despite his severe pain, hustled him into an automobile. Thus began the final month of captivity, which Blum himself described in a book. It was a long month of wandering through Germany. A convoy guarded by SS soldiers headed south and after a lengthy journey entered the camp at Flossenbürg, where Blum saw prisoners even more emaciated than those he had glimpsed in Buchenwald. There, prisoners suspected of having staged the failed attempt on Hitler's life on July 20, 1944, joined the convoy, which set out again for Regensburg. Blum and Janot spent that night in a prison cell, in which they noted traces left on the walls by prisoners awaiting execution. The next day, after a long journey, the convoy entered the concentration camp at Dachau, where Blum was moved by the sight of columns of prisoners treated like "human livestock," men and women "wearing hideous robes . . . most marching on wooden shoes."[63] As Russian troops advanced rapidly, Blum witnessed the cruel evacuation of the camp before once again heading south, still in an SS-guarded convoy, which entered Austria, moved into the Dolomites, and eventually reached Niederdorf, where a company of the Wehrmacht replaced the SS. The trucks continued along narrow mountain roads until they suddenly encountered Italian partisans and American soldiers, who liberated the prisoners. Blum's nightmare had finally come to an end.

In short order he and Janot were flown in an American aircraft from Verona to Orly, where they landed on May 14, 1945. He was expected, and a newspaper account described his arrival: "A door in the fuselage opened. Léon Blum appeared. Applause rang out, along with shouts of 'Vive Blum!' . . . Abruptly, Blum moved his hand to his lips. A gesture of affection and tenderness learned in childhood. . . . The party once again had a leader."[64] The emotion was intense. Messages of congratulation poured in from unknown schoolteachers as well as great writers, such as Saint-John Perse and Roger Martin du Gard, who wrote: "I never stopped thinking about you during those sinister years as one of their most symbolic victims. . . . Your trials have not changed you. Your honest, clear-sighted, serene intelligence is still with you as always." Nathan Netter, the grand rabbi of Metz, also sent a brief message: "A miracle has just occurred for you and all our co-religionists who managed to elude the monster, now slain at long last. May the Almighty keep you as you deserve after so many years of physical and moral suffering."[65]

Still overcome with joy, Blum learned the dreadful news that his brother René, arrested by the French police in December 1941, had died at Auschwitz, apparently burned alive. But he was reunited with his daughter-in-law Renée, who had been so devoted and courageous through the years, as well as his daughter and other family members and friends. Meanwhile, Janot learned that her son Georges Torrès had been killed in action; she was moved to tears upon meeting his young wife Tereska, wearing the uniform of the Free French, and their infant child.[66]

Soon after these family reunions came the trial of Marshal Pétain, which began in July. Blum was a key witness. He carefully prepared his testimony, which began with the riots of February 6, 1934, retraced the history of "military defeatism," recounted his departure from Paris ("I wanted to stay"), and moved on to "the shame" and "corrupting bath of Vichy . . . the fear." He described his own fate in a few lapidary phrases: "Arrested September 15. Condemned by Pétain. Delivered to Germany." He accused Pétain of "treason." The judges at the Riom trial were also "traitors" who "falsified" the record and "would have condemned us." Nevertheless, Blum remained true to his convictions: "I seek no vengeance," he wrote. "Life over the past twenty-five years prepared me for the ordeal, hardened me for combat."[67]

In September, Pierre Laval was sentenced to death after a hasty trial. Janot urged Blum to intervene, since it was thanks to Laval that she had been able to join him in Buchenwald. While awaiting the decision of the minister of justice, Blum received a long letter from Laval himself on September 22. From his cell Laval wrote: "I take the liberty of writing you in the name of relations between us which, though disrupted at times by politics and events, are so old that you may well wish to prevent the miscarriage of justice of which I am about to become the victim. . . . Because you have suffered, you will have a better sense of the injustice of delivering me without adequate defense into the hands of jurors who, the less informed they are, the more likely they are to treat me harshly. . . . To borrow an expression from your writings, 'the lock on my door and the bars on my window have not separated me from France.' I hope that they will not prevent me from believing in justice, especially when it is to you that I address this appeal." On October 12, Blum received another letter, from Laval's wife, imploring him to stop her husband's execution: "I address this appeal to you because I know your sense of justice and fairness. I know that you alone could and still can save my husband's life." Two days later, Laval sent him a final letter: "Before the irreparable is done, I send you this one final appeal. Will you help me? You can save me. There is still time. Tomorrow may be too late. I have no recourse higher than you. . . . A gesture from you would mean life for me. A refusal means death."

Blum wrote to General de Gaulle: "My dear General, I do not think capital punishment can be carried out after a trial like that one. It is a question not of pardon but of seeing that justice is done. Between us there has never been the slightest sympathy or community of views, and you know that I owe him no gratitude. But in other times I called for justice. I respect it and would ask that it be respected." He added: "I have reread this hastily written letter and am afraid that it may be ambiguous. I am asking not for a pardon but for a new trial, or, rather, a trial."[68] Blum was not heeded. Laval was executed, while plans were made for a limited purge of people who had served the Vichy regime.[69]

9

◄►◄◆►◄►

Kfar Blum

NOT FAR from the Jordan River, in a valley in Upper Galilee at the foot of snow-covered Mount Hermon, the traveler discovers a place that is like something out of a dream: quiet, lush, with neat little houses and cultivated fields as far as the eye can see and a high-tech factory that manufactures batteries for computers. Among the rocks, wreathed in flowers, is a surprising statue of Léon Blum. An inscription in Hebrew reads: "Léon Blum, head of the French government in 1936–1937." The site chosen for the Kfar Blum kibbutz, built in Blum's honor in November 1943 by a group of immigrants from Britain, the United States, Canada, and the Baltic states, was once a region of uncultivated marshland infested with malaria and devoid of roads.[1] It is today a vital symbol of the French presence in Israel.

The initiative for the project came from the American Federation of Labor. In 1937, the union, which backed the

143

Balfour Declaration, sent a delegation to Palestine. On the way it stopped in France and met with Léon Blum, who, "as a working-class leader, head of state, and Jew, repeatedly assured us of his active interest in the efforts of Jews to rebuild a national homeland. . . . That is why we sought to build an agricultural colony that would bear the name of Léon Blum."[2] A national committee was organized to solicit funds. Its chairs included Rose Schneiderman, the president of the New York Trade Union League, who, along with Clara Lemlich, had issued the Yiddish appeal that led to a celebrated strike of textile workers in 1909, a woman who so impressed Louis Brandeis that he joined the Zionist movement.[3] The creation of Kfar Blum had been made possible by a dinner to benefit the "Léon Blum Colony in Palestine," which was held in New York on December 6, 1938, under the auspices of Mrs. Franklin D. Roosevelt and the French ambassador to the United States. Some 1,500 guests attended. Among the sponsors were Herbert Lehman, the governor of New York, Fiorello La Guardia, the mayor of New York City, the writer Abraham Cahan, Albert Einstein, Supreme Court justice Felix Frankfurter, a friend of both Franklin Roosevelt and Louis Brandeis, Stephen Wise, the president of the American Jewish Congress, Solomon Goldman, the president of the Zionist Organization of America, and many other leaders of Jewish organizations.[4] William Green, the president of the American Federation of Labor, was the first to speak:

> Democracy is our safeguard against oppression and racial discrimination. . . . We vigorously protest against the persecution of Jewish people in Germany. . . . The Founders of the Léon Blum Colony in Palestine are responding to the needs of this distressing international situation . . . and to perpetuate his great name and to associate it with the cultural, educational and economic life of that part of Palestine in which the Colony is located.[5]

Count René de Saint-Quentin, the French ambassador to the United States, who attended the banquet, noted that "by naming this colony after Léon Blum, you have chosen to name it after the most patriotic citizen of this great nation, the orator and writer whose life stands as proof that in France as in the United States, anyone, regardless of his religion or any other kind of discrimination, is sure to attain the honors he deserves by virtue of his talent and his devotion to the national idea."[6] Menahem Ussishkin, the president of the Jewish National Fund, said that "from the hills and valleys of Zion, the Jewish National Fund and I congratulate you on undertaking this noble project: to create a new colony named after that great Jewish statesman, working-class leader, and champion of democracy, Léon Blum."[7] From Paris, Blum sent an emotional message:

> As a Frenchman, as a socialist and as a Jew, I feel proud at the thought that American citizens, American workers, should wish to connect my name with the establishment of an institution on the soil of Palestine, with the creation of a colony of labor in the Jewish national Home where workers will be free, where the great principles of tolerance and equity, proclaimed to the world a century and a half ago by your young Republic and our Revolution will become an enduring reality. . . . May tonight's festive occasion inspire with faith and courage the millions of Jews who today suffer, on the soil of their homeland as well as throughout the diaspora, from persecution, cruelty and oppression.[8]

Shortly thereafter, the president of the Jewish National Fund of America wrote to Blum: "Our fondest wish is that the Colony that is to be created in your name will stand as a permanent token of the spiritual bond that exists between you and Eretz Israel."[9] In honor of Blum, the following text was placed in a sealed container beneath the first stone of the first house built in the kibbutz: "We children of exile have come here from all over the world. . . . We have organized an army of workers to stand watch over the Jewish community in this newly built homeland. . . . Our village enjoys the signal privilege of bearing the name of our elder brother Léon Blum. He is a beacon to the world. . . . All his life he has been our brother. Anxious about your fate, we pray that you may emerge safe and sound from this cruel ordeal."[10] On November 10, 1943, at the Kfar Blum inauguration ceremony attended by Golda Meyerson, the future Golda Meir, Yossef Sprintzak, the future president of the Knesset, and Count Chambron, the consul general of France, Moshe Sharett, who would later become foreign minister and then prime minister of Israel, made the following statement.

> We give this kibbutz the name of a man who stands between life and death, of a man who, before our very eyes, suffers the lot of a martyr because he is a Jew, because he is a Frenchman, because he is a symbol of intellectual freedom and social justice. In the person of Léon Blum, the enthusiastic Frenchman and the Jew faithful to his traditions, French spirituality and the morality of the Jewish prophets have combined in a glorious creation of human nobility. . . . He came to us not in his days of suffering and persecution but when he was at the height of his success; and he came not in order to assume control and take over the direction of affairs but to serve the cause of the resurrection of the Jewish people as a soldier in the ranks. . . . Few Jews in the Western countries have understood as well as he the intimate significance and the absolute necessity of our work of reconstruction in Palestine. Few are the men who have seized so strongly as he the spirit of national as well as social renaissance that infuses our undertaking. . . . He spoke at Zurich as a convinced and enthusiastic Jew but he spoke, too, as a representative of humanity, of a better humanity.[11]

After World War II, Kfar Blum became a pilgrimage site for French Socialist leaders. They paid homage to the life-

sized portrait of Léon Blum that hangs in the communal din-
ing room and expressed their gratitude to kibbutz leaders.[12]

Blum made no secret of his positive attitude toward Zionism. In August 1922, for example, he presided over a rally at La
Mutualité in Paris when the mandate for Palestine was ratified:
"The Socialists of the world and we, the Socialists of France,
will do everything in our power to help you, because Zionism,
a product of class suffering, is compatible with international
socialism. Jaurès would love your work. It is socialist because it
is just, humane, and of the people."[13] A few years later, in 1925,
he sent a message for the inauguration of the Hebrew University in Jerusalem, which "doubly touched my heart as a Jew
and a Frenchman": "The new Judea will always remember the
boons of the Great Revolution, it will not forget that it was the
armies of the Republic that smashed its sons' chains. A socialist
can only hope that the renaissance of Jewish culture will yield
fine fruit."[14]

Blum's sympathy for the Zionist project was so well known
that in June 1925, Jean-Richard Bloch, identifying himself as
"both a writer and a Jew," asked Blum to help Meir Dizengoff,
"the creator, mayor, and Napoleon of Tel Aviv."[15] In 1926, Blum
became president of the French Zionist Union and was also
made an honorary member of the Pro-Palestinian Friends Circle.[16] In 1928, he published a long article in the journal *Palestine:*
"The Jewish national homeland exists politically and interna-
tionally in a way that sets it apart from other parts of Palestine. It
was planted, or, rather, replanted, with a status of its own. It
has begun to play, and will increasingly play, an original role, a
peacemaking role. . . . If one wants to see the national homeland really take hold in the midst of 700,000 Arabs, it will be
necessary to send 20 to 25,000 new settlers to Palestine every
year for the next ten or fifteen years, some 250 to 300,000 in
all. . . . A loan therefore seems essential, if only as a comple-
ment to voluntary gifts." This loan was to be guaranteed by the

great powers.[17] In July 1929, the Sixteenth Zionist Congress convened in Zurich at the same time as an important meeting of the Jewish Agency, and Chaim Weizmann therefore urged Blum to come to Zurich to deliver an important speech. "I realize," he wrote, "how valuable your time is given your position in public life, but the circumstances are exceptional, so I hope you will be able to accept this invitation." Marc Jarblum, a Socialist leader and Zionist who was close to Blum, went to Divonne-les-Bains, where Blum was vacationing, and drove him to Zurich, where his speech was given a triumphal reception. It included these words: "I am Zionist because I am French, Jewish, and Socialist, because modern Jewish Palestine represents a unique and unprecedented encounter between humanity's oldest traditions and its boldest and most recent search for liberty and social justice."[18]

Blum and Weizmann had known and admired each other for several years. Their first meeting seems to have taken place during World War I, when the French government, seeking to persuade the United States to intervene in the war, sent a delegation to meet with Jewish Americans thought to have influence with the government. A preliminary meeting was held at Marcel Sembat's justice ministry. Among those in attendance were Victor Basch, the old Dreyfusard and friend of Blum, who was to head the delegation, Marc Jarblum, and André Blumel, Sembat's chief of staff.[19] To everyone's astonishment, Blum demonstrated detailed knowledge of Zionist issues and turned out to be quite positively disposed toward the Zionist project. Jarblum then put Blum in contact with Weizmann. Their friendship continued to grow from then until the death of the Zionist leader who was destined to become the first president of the State of Israel. It has been said that Weizmann literally "enlisted" Blum in the Zionist cause.[20] The two met often, both publicly and privately, and saw each other constantly.[21] Their wives shared their friendship. In 1922, at the time of the

Peace Conference, Blum facilitated Weizmann's contacts with the French prime minister, Raymond Poincaré. Whenever Weizmann visited Paris, he met with Blum and through him was introduced to any number of French political leaders. At the time of the Balfour Declaration, he counted on Blum to influence the French position. On October 5, 1926, Weizmann participated in a London meeting of the Zionist Economic Conference. He wrote the following note, which attests to the close relationship and mutual confidence between the two men: "Blum should let me know when he arrives and whom he would like to see (Macdonald or others). I can arrange all that. I expect him to stay with me, and I will meet him at the station if I know exactly when he will arrive. This meeting is so important that he might want to postpone some of his other obligations."[22]

Meanwhile, the Blum-Weizmann dialogue grew deeper. Weizmann begged Blum to intervene with his friends in the British Labour Party to protest British-imposed limits on Jewish immigration to Palestine. In his words, "Blum was embarrassed to learn how his comrades were behaving, and it seems this will make him a better Zionist."[23] Later, Blum wrote: "I judged [Weizmann's] extraordinary influence on others by his influence on me. I have never been able to refuse him anything."[24] His own role as head of government led Blum to act promptly, not only in 1936 during the Popular Front but also in late 1946, when for a brief period he again served as prime minister. In March 1936, Weizmann met Blum to discuss anti-Jewish actions taken by the mufti of Jerusalem. He wanted Blum to pressure the English to contact the Quai d'Orsay, which seemed to be protecting the mufti. In July 1936, Weizmann asked Blum to persuade the British to moderate their repressive policies in Palestine. Somewhat later, Blum, facing a threat of strikes, had to excuse himself from attending a meeting of the Jewish National Fund in Paris. He nevertheless met

with Weizmann while the Matignon Accords were being negotiated.[25] Clearly, even in this period of turmoil at home, he did
not lose sight of the plight of Palestine and the difficulties of
Jewish immigration.

In a more direct statement of the connection between his
destiny as a French Jew and that of the newly created state of
Israel, Blum had this to say at a ceremony honoring his friend
Weizmann, who had just been elected president of Israel:

> I knew nothing about Zionism when I met him. He intro-
> duced me to the work and won me over. After World War
> I, he enlisted me in his designs and occasionally sought my
> advice. . . . Although I am a French Jew, born in France to a
> long line of French ancestors, and speak no language other
> than that of my country; and although I refused to leave
> France even when I was in great danger, I nevertheless share
> with all my soul in your admirable efforts, which have been
> miraculously transformed from a dream into a historical re-
> ality. From now on, every Jew can be sure of finding equality
> and liberty in a worthy homeland, even those not fortunate
> as I was to find these things in the land of their birth. I have
> followed these efforts ever since President Weizmann first
> made me aware of them. I have always supported them and
> support them today more than ever.[26]

Blum often referred to himself as a "French Jew," deeply
assimilated, proud of his ancestors and of his thorough integration in the fatherland of the Revolution. He was the archetype of the "state Jew," both a *normalien* and a member of
the Council of State, as well as a prestigious intellectual and
friend of Jaurès, Barrès, and Gide. He was the quintessence of
Frenchness, who boasted of his inability to express himself in
any tongue other than his native French. Yet he singlehandedly
tried to transform the relation between French Judaism and
Zionism. Consider, for example, the letter sent to him from
London on April 8, 1932, by the Jewish Agency for Palestine on

the occasion of his sixtieth birthday: "We will always remember with gratitude your important services to Palestine and to the Jewish people, and it is for us a great joy to be able to count in the future as in the past on your warm sympathy and powerful and generous support."[27]

In contrast to Blum's support for Zionism, most French Jewish leaders were for a long time hesitant if not hostile. Many of the best known and most influential state Jews outright opposed the Zionist project. Joseph Reinach, for example, who played a key role in the early years of the Third Republic, wrote that "if by Zionism one means the constitution of a Jewish state in Palestine, I say clearly, No. . . . The mere idea of a religiously based state is contrary to all the principles of the modern world. . . . Since there is no such thing as a Jewish race or Jewish nation and there is only a Jewish religion, Zionism is a foolish idea, a threefold error—historical, archeological, and ethnic."[28] Unlike Blum, Reinach believed that Zionism was antithetical to the French idea of a community of citizens. In his view, support for Zionism would separate Jews from the nation; they would become members of another nation or a particular race. His brother Théodore Reinach, an eminent academic, contributor to the *Revue des Études Juives*, and founder of the liberal synagogue, argued similarly that "the Zionist enterprise will be disastrous if it fails and even more disastrous if, against all probability, it succeeds. . . . Drumont will then have been right. . . . Anti-Semitism lurks on all sides. . . . If Judaism becomes an official nationality, the Jews of France will have to choose between Judaism and France."[29] Most French Jewish leaders shared this view, which was in fact Drumont's. The pope of French anti-Semitism made no secret of his enthusiasm for Zionism, because it cast doubt on the integration of Jews into French society, which he vehemently condemned. He and his supporters made speech after speech applauding pro-Zionist statements: for them, the return of the Jews to

Zion would be a blessing, their dream come true, as their oft-repeated slogan made clear: "France for the French," and the Jews to Palestine.[30]

At the turn of the twentieth century, Zionism found few supporters in France other than Bernard Lazare and a few Jewish immigrants, essentially because it was so at odds with the universalist ideals of the French Revolution, which the vast majority of French Jews fully embraced. Both the Alliance Israélite Universelle and the Consistory rejected the Jewish nationalist ideas of Theodore Herzl. Grand Rabbi Zadoc Kahn asked, "if none of its civil, political, or religious laws is Jewish, why would the new state call itself a Jewish state?"[31] Leading French Jews such as Sylvain Lévi, who had the ear of the Quai d'Orsay, were afraid of being accused of dual allegiances and therefore condemned Weizmann, who in return branded Lévi a "traitor." After the massacre of Jews in Palestine in 1929, however, which Blum, as a socialist, saw through the lens of class struggle and blamed solely on Arab landlords, a number of Jewish leaders previously hostile to Zionism began to feel greater sympathy for the movement.[32] Alfred Berl nevertheless continued to believe that the birth of a Jewish state would be "a lamentable disavowal of the great principles laid down by the generous minds and noble thinkers of the eighteenth century and the French Revolution, people like Mendelssohn, Mirabeau, Grégoire, and Clermont-Tonnerre."[33]

Yet as early as 1917, André Spire, a colleague of Blum's at the Council of State, took the initiative in creating the Ligue des Amis du Sionisme (Friends of Zionism League), which included non-Jewish members in addition to writers and poets such as Gustave Kahn, Jean-Richard Bloch, Edmond Fleg, and Jules Isaac, who also joined the France-Palestine Association, created in 1925, of which Blum was a member as well.[34] They were not afraid to participate in the activities of the Jewish National Fund (KKL) or to write in its newspaper *La Terre Retrou-*

vée.[35] But none of them showed the slightest desire to abandon France or move to Palestine, to "make *aliyah.*" Edmond Fleg, discussing his memories of the Third Zionist Congress in Basel, wrote in 1928: "I felt Jewish, very Jewish, but I also felt very French, Genevan but French. . . . The Jewish homeland beckoned only to those Jews who did not think they had any other."[36] Similarly, André Spire saw himself as a "champion" of immigrant Jews but remained a "Frenchman of longstanding" devoted to his country.[37] These proponents of philanthropic Zionism were simply interested in helping stateless Jews who wanted to settle in Palestine.[38]

To be sure, it is possible to argue that Blum's pro-Zionist statements reveal a state of mind similar to that of Spire and other French Jews; in other words, he spoke out in favor of Zionism as "a French Jew," as he put it. Even if he participated with "all [his] soul" in the effort to build a Jewish homeland, Blum never envisioned leaving his native land. His action nevertheless marked a turn toward a Zionism that was more political than philanthropic—an important change in French Judaism, which no longer feared the horrendous climate of the Dreyfus Affair with its accusations of treason and dual allegiance. For the first time, perhaps, in the history of France, a state Jew of unquestioned legitimacy publicly took a remarkably courageous stand, insisting on a more complex idea of citizenship based on multiple but noncontradictory allegiances. Blum, a quintessential representative of the most sophisticated Frenchness, did not hesitate to argue that Jews without a homeland were free to invent one for themselves. Although in 1925 he wrote that "a socialist can only hope for the fine fruit to be expected from a renaissance of Jewish culture" and affirmed in a speech that "Zionism was not originally a national demand and still is not one today," in 1948 he spoke out in favor of a "homeland" open to all Jews without one.[39]

His stance in this period is reminiscent of that of Louis

Brandeis, a deeply assimilated American Jew who became a Zionist after encountering immigrant Jewish strikers. As the first Jew appointed to the Supreme Court, in 1916, Brandeis continued to take part in Zionist rallies. "I have gradually become aware that in order to be good Americans, we must be better Jews, and to be better Jews, we must become Zionists." Furthermore: "Every American Jew who aids in advancing the Jewish settlement in Palestine, though he feels that neither he nor his descendants will ever live there, will likewise be a better man and a better American for doing so. There is no inconsistency between loyalty to America and loyalty to Jewry."[40] Blum, at the Council of State, and Brandeis, at the Supreme Court, were both national and international figures who spoke out in favor of Zionism, in contrast to the German foreign minister Walter Rathenau, who by Chaim Weizmann's account made no secret of his active hostility.[41] Brandeis, however, supported a cultural Zionism similar to that of Ahad Ha'am, and when the more political position of his friend Weizmann won out, his ardor cooled. By contrast, Blum moved easily from cultural and philanthropic Zionism to political Zionism: after World War II, he backed Weizmann's urgent call for a Jewish state in Palestine. Brandeis, a proponent of American pluralism, hoped that a Jewish presence in Palestine could coexist, as in the United States, with other collective identities. Blum instead envisioned a French-type state, strongly centralized and secularized, in the Middle East.

Barely ten days after returning from captivity, Blum, hoping to contribute to the birth of the Jewish state, met Marc Jarblum over lunch to discuss the affairs of the World Jewish Committee. On November 11, 1945, soldiers from the Jewish Brigade in Palestine came to Paris to honor Jewish soldiers killed in World War II. After David Ben-Gurion called for the creation of a Jewish state, someone read a statement from Blum:

"I am excited by the Jewish Brigade's heroic struggle for the just cause of humanity and the Jewish people. I hope that your aspirations are realized and that the gates of Palestine will be opened to unlimited immigration."[42] Later, in 1946, he sent a message to the Histadrut (the Israeli trade union organization): "I am pleased once again to express my steadfast sympathy for the working class of Israel, which is working to build socialism and to set an example of inestimable value to the working class of the entire world."[43] He also defended the Haganah (the Jewish paramilitary organization in Palestine), pointing out that "one inevitably provokes in courageous young men the state of mind characterized as terrorist when one places them in a situation without prospects or hope."[44]

On June 20, 1946, he received a letter from Jarblum, who still headed the Jewish Agency for Palestine, asking him to write urgently to British prime minister Clement Attlee and foreign minister Ernest Bevin: "In this way you will help to improve relations between Palestine and Great Britain." Jarblum also urged him to send telegrams to the Socialist Zionist Conference (Poale Sion) in Paris, which Blum did at once: "Follow with great interest splendid efforts. Am certain will overcome all difficulties and ultimately build a fine Jewish Palestine. Fraternal greetings."[45] On July 2, Blum was invited to take part with Ben-Gurion in a demonstration against British obstruction of the Zionist project, organized by the central committee of French Zionists. A few days later, he received a long letter from the president of the Zionist Organization of France urging him to take a stand against Britain's policy.[46] He met Ben-Gurion on several occasions and defended Jewish emigrants intercepted by the British on their way to Palestine. "Will force be used," he asked, "to drive out of Palestine those who have been bringing the dead land back to life there for the past forty years?"[47] Furthermore: "How can it be that the survivors of the

Lublin and Warsaw ghettos and the orphans of Jews gassed at Auschwitz are being denied admission to the place they sought to build a new homeland?"[48]

His commitment to Zionism was such that, in the face of Arab resistance to Jewish settlement, he was suspected of "having signed with the Americans" an agreement so that "the excess Jews of other nations would be directed to France" rather than Palestine.[49] During a brief stint as prime minister in late 1946, Blum strongly urged that Jewish refugees from Prague be admitted to Palestine. In a note to the minister of the interior, he wrote: "The French position in this type of affair remains unchanged. We do not need to verify the sincerity of the entry visas presented to us."[50] Blum received letters from anonymous writers, one of whom wrote: "I hope that M. Léon Blum, after devoting his life to the interests of his country and of socialism, will devote himself to his miserable brethren. . . . Be a good Jew, M. Blum. For us there is no greater duty."[51]

During the summer of 1947, Blum vigorously defended the passengers on the *Exodus*, the ship that left Sète in July bound for Palestine with 4,500 displaced persons aboard, many of them camp survivors, including numerous orphans. After being intercepted by British forces, the passengers were unceremoniously returned to Germany. Blum wrote a number of pro-Zionist articles for *Le Populaire*. "The passengers aboard the *Exodus* are not terrorists," he wrote. "They are simply martyrs. They would die with arms in hand, as heroes, like their fathers and brothers, mothers and sisters, of the Warsaw ghetto." "Pardon the unlucky heroes of the *Exodus!* The ship's passengers are not crates that longshoremen can pass from hand to hand, freight to be unloaded indiscriminately in this port or that depot. They are human beings, free individuals." In his final article, Blum repeated words he had used in other solemn moments:

I was born a Jew. For 25 years I have done my best to help build a "national home" in Palestine, and I have never thought of leaving France. Why do the Jews of the *Exodus*, Jews from the German camps who are eagerly reaching out to Palestine, nearly all come from a country where there is no free government and where anti-Semitic persecution preceded Hitlerian extermination? Because after such ordeals, they dream of asylum in a land that would be partly their own. . . . They naturally, legitimately, aspire to refuge in a homeland. . . . We must understand, we must accept, that they have every reason today to seek that homeland on biblical ground, on the land of their history, on land that for half a century Jews previously driven out by persecution, who await them, have drained, cultivated, improved, and caused to bloom with their own hands.[52]

In this context, Édouard Depreux, then minister of the interior and close to Blum, put André Blumel officially in charge of assisting the ship's passengers. (A "Depreux Grove" would later be planted in Palestine as a token of gratitude for this action.)

In 1947, the partition of Palestine into two states was under consideration. The traditionally pro-Arab Quai d'Orsay did not hide its firm opposition to this plan. Several officials charged with defending French interests in the region were openly hostile. The consul general of France in Jerusalem described Zionist militants as "fundamentally racist—at least as racist as their German persecutors and in spite of their democratic leaning. These Jews are increasingly inclined to treat their common religious particularism as a rallying point for the divergent national and racial tendencies created in the Diaspora. . . . Once the Jew becomes master, he leaves no doubt about the future that non-Israelis would face in an independent Jewish state."[53] In November 1947, Weizmann contacted Blum late one night to urge him to intervene. His longtime friends Blumel and Jarblum joined him in trying to make sure that the French position at the United Nations would favor the creation of the state of Israel. They met with Vincent Auriol, the president of the Republic, in an attempt to halt the delaying tactics of the ministry of foreign affairs. In the same month, Léon Askenazi, known as Manitou, took a group of his students from the School of Young Jewish Leadership, a celebrated Jewish seminary in Orsay, to meet Blum at Jouy-en-Josas shortly before the vote on the resolution to divide Palestine, urging him to act.[54]

On October 25, 1947, Blum ignored thinly veiled threats from French Muslim deputies and the Arab League and sent a long letter to Georges Bidault, then foreign minister, arguing that an abstention by France would be "bad news," "an injustice [showing] lack of courage," especially since "a continuation of the vague status quo will not prevent clashes and bloodshed."[55] He also contacted Vincent Auriol: "Nothing is worse for us, from the standpoint of our North African territories, than a sign of weakness and fear in the face of pro-Arab fanaticism."[56] Weizmann telephoned again to ask him to urge the new prime minister, Robert Schuman, to consider the justice of the Zionist position. At a meeting of the council of ministers, interior minister Jules Moch and labor minister Daniel Mayer opposed a French abstention in the upcoming U.N. vote. All of these men were at pains to show that their efforts on behalf of the Zionist movement did not depend on their being Jewish.[57] This was not enough to prevent anti-Semites from objecting. In January 1948, for example, an anonymous individual wrote the Prefect: "Follow the words and actions of M. L. Blum and his people. Because M. Blum, like all Jews, is very dangerous. France has no need of such dangerous foreigners in its midst. Act quickly before it is too late. A true Frenchman."[58]

Other non-Jewish friends such as Vincent Auriol, André Philip, and Édouard Depreux also worked on behalf of the Zionist movement. Close to Blum, all these men played a vital role in bringing about the final French vote in favor of partition. In February 1948, Weizmann again consulted Blum about whether a Jewish state should be proclaimed immediately. Without hesitation Blum responded that immediate action was imperative.[59] In May the question of recognizing the new state came up. The Quai d'Orsay was opposed, and there was strong pressure against recognition from Arab governments, which openly threatened France with reprisals if it recognized Israel. Blum said, "It's now or never."[60] On May 14 he sent a telegram to Ben-Gurion: "In this grave and promising moment made possible by the courageous pioneers of Jewish Palestine, I wish to express my admiration and profound sympathy. I heartily wish you success in your splendid efforts to build a Jewish state based on social justice, which will be an important factor for peace in the Middle East and the world."[61] The Socialist Party central committee itself urged "the government of the French Republic to recognize the new state without delay." After months of discussion, recognition finally came in January 1949.

Conclusion: Finishing Touches

UPON RETURNING from Buchenwald, Blum once again took up the torch of democratic socialism in a context soon marked by the Cold War, confrontation with the Soviet Union, and a new hard line from the Communists, with whom Blum saw eye-to-eye about nothing. Nor did he share the views of General de Gaulle's supporters. Although he had been a loyal ally of de Gaulle throughout the war, he now feared that the general's partisans would encourage him to assert his personal power. Eager to maintain a regime of parliamentary sovereignty, Blum rejected the conclusion of de Gaulle's Bayeux speech, which proposed entrusting all power to the chief executive. Instead, he sought to strengthen the party system, which he believed essential to a vital democracy. In the November 1946 legislative elections, however, the Communist Party for the first time garnered more votes than the Socialist Party. Blum saw his ideas for a moral regeneration of socialism and his desire to reject reductive Marxism contested within the party itself by Guy Mollet, who, to Blum's dismay, became master of "the old house." Blum's place in the Fourth Republic became uncertain; his voice no longer made itself heard.

In February 1946 he was sent to the United States as ambassador to negotiate reconstruction financing with the Americans. He delivered a number of speeches in New York and Washington before moving on to Canada to negotiate a similar deal with the Canadians.[1] In December 1946, he was again chosen, almost unanimously, to serve as prime minister. During his short term in office, he took steps to revive economic modernization through "the Plan," and as a consistent advocate of independence for France's colonies he sought to avoid being drawn into war in Indochina. Everyone praised his patriotism, his "sacrifice" for the nation.[2] In late January 1947, however, Blum lost his majority, and the experiment ended prematurely. In November 1947, in a period of great political instability and social polarization, Blum, hoping to embody a "third way" between Communism and Gaullism, agreed once again to stand as a candidate for prime minister. This time he failed, however. His political career had come to an end.

Blum and Janot, his wife, retired to Jouy-en-Josas, where they lived in a nice, quiet house surrounded by flowers. Blum stood back from active life and began to write, while responding to numerous requests for advice. Among his late texts, we find his final homage, written in February 1950, to his friend Chaim Weizmann, who had become Israel's first president: "I have always felt myself in solidarity with you, and I feel more so now than ever." He also wrote an article, which appeared shortly after his death, in which he expressed his wish that Jerusalem should remain the capital of Israel.[3] In these final months of his life, the stands he took on many issues attest to the intensity of his commitment to Israel, which historians have all too often ignored. In *Forward*, a socialist newspaper

symbolic of Jewish life in the diaspora, with which he had considered working "as a Jew" in the interwar period, he worked
out a parallel between Jewish history and German history in a
text of high moral seriousness that captured his lifelong commitment.[4]

> I refuse to make the slightest concession to racial concepts in
> the name of which millions of Jews have been tortured and
> exterminated. I do not accept the collective guilt and collec-
> tive punishment of entire peoples. I do not place the slight-
> est credence in allegedly indelible ethnic characteristics as the
> basis for a curse of inhumanity, cruelty, and barbarism against
> any people. Peoples are changed and transformed by the ma-
> terial, political, cultural, and moral conditions to which they
> are subjected. The Hitlerian regime did not establish a per-
> manent German character any more than the ghettos of the
> East established a permanent Semitic character. . . . Since
> the time of the prophets, for nearly 2,000 years, Israel has
> known what the dogma of collective responsibility can cost
> a people. . . . I do not believe in the collective responsibility
> of peoples, whether it be the German people or the Jewish
> people. . . . Nor do I believe in the permanence of racial
> types. . . . In the most recent world crisis, the Jewish people
> have undoubtedly endured the bloodiest sacrifice. Perhaps
> that sacrifice is in some mysterious way linked to a new ser-
> vice that Jews must perform for humankind.[5]

In his final days, Blum proclaimed his faith in individual
freedom and rejected the kind of ethnic determinism that had
been used to condemn the Jews in the past and was now being
used to condemn Germans. He unambiguously affirmed the
existence of a Jewish people, represented by the "young Israeli
pioneers" whose project of national renovation he had so ardently supported. His conclusion is nevertheless strange: the
"bloody sacrifice" of the Jews is "in some mysterious way linked
to a new service" to humankind. Such a quasi-mystical vocabu-

lary seems inappropriate to describe the extermination of Jews who hardly thought of themselves as making a "sacrifice."

Blum's health deteriorated rapidly. On March 30, 1950, he died of a heart attack. The news was greeted with an intense outpouring of emotion: a national figure, the heir of Jaurès, the leader of the Popular Front, whose social messianism, whatever its limits, had so profoundly transformed French society, was gone. The funeral procession began in Jouy-en-Josas. Blum's body, preceded by a squad of motorcycle police, entered Paris via the Porte d'Orléans and proceeded to Denfert-Rochereau, down the Boulevard Saint-Michel and the Rue de Rivoli to the Avenue de l'Opéra and Rue Lafayette before pausing in front of the offices of *Le Populaire*, the newspaper that Blum had edited for so many years. Spotlights illuminated the coffin, covered with red cloth, while young socialists wearing blue shirts and red ties formed an honor guard around it. The people of Paris filed past the remains of this extraordinary man—at once effeminate and virile, an admirer of Stendhal, an aesthete and a friend of Barrès who had known Proust and accompanied Alfred Cortot, a man with a melodious voice and fragile appearance who had nevertheless been an adept of dueling, a Jew who loved women as well as literature, a statesman who, from the Dreyfus Affair to Vichy through two world wars had experienced all the tragedies of modern France, a revolutionary dedicated to reform, an internationalist patriot dedicated to peace, a leader with whom the masses could identify, and an eminent defender of the fatherland in its darkest hours who never made a secret of his commitment to Zionism. Then, preceded by a hundred miners from Pas-de-Calais wearing their blue work clothes and miner's lamps and by three hundred red flags knotted as a sign of mourning, while a brass band played the "Internationale," the procession continued toward the Place de la Concorde. As Blum's old friend Vincent Auriol, now president of the Republic, looked on, the carefully organized national funeral ceremony unfolded under an icy, pouring rain. Troops marched past a reviewing stand where numerous invited guests had assembled, while bands played Socialist Party songs.[6]

An emotional France celebrated the memory of the great man it had just lost. Politicians and union leaders deplored his passing. The years of disagreement and invective were forgotten, although the Communist Party refused to participate in the funeral and did not shrink from publishing a bitterly hostile portrait of Blum.[7] Old friends wrote to Janot. André Gide telegraphed his condolences in staccato phrases: "deeply saddened by end ever deeper and warmer friendship."[8] Roger Martin du Gard, Jean Rostand, Jacques Maritain, Saint-John Perse, and Edgar Milhaud all sent messages, as did political leaders from around the world. International unions and working-class parties from many countries sent telegrams. The Spanish were well represented, a sign that the polemic about Blum's stance during the Spanish Civil War was finally over. Indalecio Prieto, the former socialist minister of defense in the Republican government, sent his fraternal condolences, while the Union of Spanish Workers wept for Blum and Spaniards in the Decazeville section of the Socialist Party "silently doffed their hats in honor of [their] illustrious companion." Spaniards living in exile in Morocco "bowed respectfully before this irreparable loss to international socialism," while the Spanish Workers' Party saluted their "great comrade Léon Blum," and Spanish refugees in France deplored "the cruel loss of a man who devoted his life to the defense of every just and humane cause." Meanwhile, Pietro Nenni wrote that he had "never forgotten the debt of gratitude" he felt toward Blum "for the friendship he displayed for us during a long exile." Similarly, the Cadore Calvi Partisan Brigade, the Free Czechoslovakian Council, the Free Polish Council, and a group of Italians banished during the fascist years all sent telegrams of condolence.

Le Populaire also gave prominence to telegrams from Israel, including one from Histadrut declaring that "France has lost a distinguished citizen, the progressive forces of the world have lost a tireless champion, the French worker's movement a wise leader, and Israel and Histadrut a faithful friend." The Mapai (Israel Workers' Party) wrote that "we admired the perfect balance he achieved between the purest tradition of humanism and the noblest legacy of Israel's prophets," while the Bund "expressed the pain of the Jewish socialist masses, cruelly afflicted." In Jouy-en-Josas, Janot received a mountain of telegrams. Among them were messages from Vera and Chaim Weizmann, "deeply distraught," and Nahum Goldmann, who wrote that Blum "will remain one of the greatest figures in the history of the world and of the Jewish people. . . . He always had a profound interest in the fate of the Jewish people." The editor of *Forward* wrote: "Sadness and despair here. Léon Blum was the most remarkable statesman of our generation." Condolences poured in from Jewish communities in North Africa, including a telegram from the chief judge of the High Rabbinical Court of Rabat, who "weeps for this loss felt by Judaism the world over." General Claude Kelman, the head of the Federation of French Jewish Societies, wrote: "Judaism suffers cruelly from the death of a great French statesman and Jew proud of his origins." Isaac Schneersohn, the head of the Jewish Documentation Center, wrote that he was "deeply saddened by the death of a great Frenchman and great Jew, Léon Blum." The Zionist Federation of France offered its condolences on behalf of "all the Zionists of France." L'Oeuvre de Secours aux Enfants (OSE, the Children's Aid Society) deplored the death of Léon Blum, calling him a "great friend of Jewish children." The children and staff of the Home for Hidden Jewish Children in Moissac also wrote.[9]

Today, however, the memory of Léon Blum is slowly fading. A relative consensus has emerged concerning his eminent place in the history of modern France, although some argue that the deep and quasi-messianic reforms of the Popular Front were not enough to overcome the Great Depression or cope with the growing fascist threat, while others mock Blum's stubborn legalism and pacifism and remain critical of his relatively passive attitude during the Spanish Civil War. Although Blum has not achieved the stature of a "great man," he is not absent from the pages of history books. A Blum museum has been created in his former home in Jouy-en-Josas.[10] Here and there a lycée or a street has been named after him. On December 10, 1956, following a debate in which certain Paris city councilors recalled the violent dissent aroused by the Popular Front, a large majority voted to rename the Place Voltaire, between République and Nation in a working-class neighborhood that Blum represented in the Chamber of Deputies, the Place Léon Blum.[11]

This consensus is nevertheless marred by some belated whiffs of the old anti-Semitism. The 1960 edition of the Larousse Dictionary, a standard reference at the time, repeated accusations from the 1930s that Blum's real name was Karfulkenstein. This caused an enormous scandal, and Larousse was condemned by the Tribunal de Grande Instance (superior court) of Paris.[12] As if to make amends for this affront many years later, a bronze statue depicting a Blum recognizable only by his glasses and all wrapped up in himself was installed in 1991 on the Place Léon Blum. Numerous official delays and rejections had preceded this event, and political fears were openly avowed. Unfortunately, on June 21, 2007, after an evening concert, a street cleaning vehicle owned by the city of Paris struck the statue and knocked it from its pedestal. Some months later, it was back in place in this working-class neighborhood of the capital, far from the brightly lit boulevards and famous monuments. Just as it had proved impossible to erect a statue of Dreyfus at the École Militaire, so that in the end it had to be put in a small square on the Boulevard Raspail where almost no one sees it, and just as the statue of Pierre Mendès-France languishes in solitude in the Jardin du Luxembourg, universally ignored, so, too, did Blum's statue suffer through any number of vicissitudes before coming to rest in this obscure place.[13] As if, in spite of his central place in the history of contemporary France, Léon Blum remained even today a figure who elicits contradictory reactions, as if his half-toned portrait might be expected to evoke doubts about a personality shaped by multiple loyalties, all of which nevertheless contributed to the fulfillment of the nation's destiny and to the achievement of justice in all its forms.

Introduction

1. *Journal officiel*, debates in the Chamber of Deputies, June 6, 1936.

2. Ibid., session of January 11, 1923. In an attempt to end this incident, the deputy Léon Archambaud declared that "it is deplorable to see this revival of religious disputes. People are as entitled to be Jewish as they are to be Protestant or Catholic." When the session chair refused to allow the use of the word "Jew," the right-wing newspaper *Action Française* proposed to refer to Blum as *le Youpin* (the Yid) or *le Youtre* (the Kike). *L'Action Française*, June 7, 1936.

3. For the alternate transcript, see Tal Bruttmann and Laurent Joly, *La France antijuive de 1936* (Paris: Editions des Equateurs, 2006), pp. 74–77.

4. Léon Daudet, "Le cabinet Blum et la question juive," *L'Action Française*, May 17, 1936.

5. On June 17, 1936, Louis Darquier de Pellepoix attacked

Léon Blum and proposed to take away the civil and political rights of Jews. *Bulletin Municipal*, June 23, 1936. In May 1942, Darquier de Pellepoix replaced Xavier Vallat as head of the General Commissariat for Jewish Questions, where he would implement an even more extreme policy of persecution than Vallat's. Vallat did not let things rest there. Somewhat later, on March 21, 1940, "a loud altercation" broke out between him and Léon Blum in the Conference Room of the Chamber of Deputies. When Vallat accused Blum of being responsible for the country's situation, Blum moved toward him "with threatening gestures," while other legislators quickly intervened to prevent "the discussion from degenerating into fisticuffs." Archives de la Préfecture de Police (Archives of the Prefecture of Police), Paris (hereinafter cited as APP), BA 1978.

6. Emmanuel Lévinas, *Humanisme de l'autre homme* (Paris: Fata Morgana, 1972), pp. 46–47.

7. Shulamit Volkov, *Walther Rathenau: Weimar's Fallen Statesman* (New Haven: Yale University Press, 2012), p. 47.

8. James Joll, *Three Intellectuals in Politics* (London: Weidenfeld and Nicolson, 1960), p. xii. Jacob Talmon, *Essais de méditation historique* (in Hebrew) (Jerusalem: Schocken, 1964), p. 241, notwithstanding, Disraeli, Rathenau, and Blum thus had different fates.

9. The American anti-Semite in question was Robert Edmonson, an organizer of the Pan-Aryan Conference, quoted in Pierre Birnbaum, *Les deux maisons: Essai sur la citoyenneté des Juifs en France et aux États-Unis* (Paris: Gallimard, 2012), p. 204.

10. Quoted in Mehmet Asci, *L'État laïque et sa religion officielle*, doctoral dissertation in political science, University of Paris I, February 2014, p. 26.

Chapter 1. Portrait of a Young Jew

1. Paula Hyman, *The Emancipation of the Jews of Alsace: Acculturation and Tradition in the Nineteenth Century* (New Haven: Yale University Press, 1991).

2. Nancy Green, *The Pletzl of Paris: Jewish Immigrant Workers in the Belle Epoque* (New York: Holmes and Meier, 1986).

3. Quoted in Ilan Greilsammer, *Léon Blum* (Paris: Flammarion, 1996), p. 25.

4. Geoffrey Fraser and Thadée Natanson, *Léon Blum: Man and Statesman* (Philadelphia: Lippincott, 1938), p. 39.

5. Pierre Birnbaum, *Jewish Destinies: Citizenship, State, and Community in Modern France* (New York: Hill and Wang, 2000), chap. 4.

6. Léon Blum, "Nouvelles conversations de Goethe avec Eckermann," in *L'oeuvre de Léon Blum, 1891–1905* (Paris: Albin Michel, 1954), p. 266.

7. Blum Archives, Fondation Nationale des Sciences Politiques (FNSP, National Foundation for Political Science, Sciences-Po), Paris (hereinafter cited as Moscow Archives), inventory 4, dossier 34, document 119.

8. In a letter to his wife Lise, he wrote of eating a "traditional *choucroute*" in a famous restaurant, Le Crocodile. Moscow Archives, inventory 4, dossier 46. Later, in 1942, while imprisoned by the Vichy regime at Bourrassol, he expressed pleasure at receiving a "lovely ham hock."

9. Quoted in Greilsammer, *Blum*, p. 31.

10. Erving Goffman, *The Presentation of Self in Everyday Life* (New York: Anchor, 1959).

11. Colette Audry, *Léon Blum ou la politique du Juste* (Paris: Julliard, 1955), pp. 13–14.

12. Léon Blum, "Souvenirs sur l'Affaire," in *L'oeuvre de Léon Blum, 1937–1940* (Paris: Albin Michel, 1965), p. 574.

13. Vivian Mann and Richard Cohen, eds., *From Court Jews to the Rothschilds: Art, Patronage, and Power, 1600–1800* (New York: Prestel, 1996).

14. *L'Oeuvre*, September 29, 1936.

15. Gustave Téry, *Vie de M Léon Blum* (Paris: L'Action publique, 1936), p. 4.

16. Jean-Pierre Maxence, *Histoire de dix ans* (Paris: Gallimard, 1936), p. 361.

17. Léon Daudet, *Termites parlementaires* (Paris: Editions du Capitole, 1930), p. 190.

18. Henri Béraud, *Popu-Roi* (Paris: Editions de France, 1938), p. 115.

19. Pierre Gaxotte, "L'homme maudit," *Candide*, April 7, 1938.

20. See, for example, *L'Humanité*, July 26, 1925.

21. Maurice Thorez, "Léon Blum tel qu'il est," *L'Internationale Socialiste*, no. 2, February 1940.

22. Simone Le Bargy, *Sous de nouveaux soleils* (Paris: Gallimard, 1957), p. 76.

23. Alfred Fabre-Luce, *Vingt-cinq années de liberté* (Paris: Julliard, 1962), p. 114; Pierre Birnbaum, *Anti-Semitism in France* (Oxford: Basil Blackwell, 1992), chap. 7. On Proust and Blum, see also *Candide*, December 12, 1935.

24. See, for example, *Correspondance de Marcel Proust*, intro. by Philip Kolb (Paris: Plon, 1979), vol. 6, p. 136.

25. Ilan Greilsammer, "Note sur une lettre inédite adressée par Marcel Proust à Léon Blum à l'époque du *Banquet*," in "Marcel Proust 5: Proust au tournant du siècle," ed. Bernard Brun and Juliette Hassine, *La Revue des Lettres Modernes* (2005), p. 10.

26. Paul-Henri Bourrelier, *La Revue Blanche: Une génération dans l'engagement, 1890–1905* (Paris: Fayard, 2007), pp. 445, 447.

27. Léon Blum, "Declamatio suasoria," in *Cahiers Leon Blum*, "Léon Blum avant Léon Blum, Les années litteraires," nos. 23–25, 1988, p. 106.

28. Marcel Proust, *Correspondance*, vol. 19, p. 575. Proust's friend the Jewish composer Reynaldo Hahn, who was also close to Léon Blum, wrote: "Today, Marcel fought with Jean Lorrain, who wrote an odious article about him in the *Journal*. He remained cool and steadfast for three days, which struck me as incompatible with his nerves but did not surprise me at all." Reynaldo Hahn, Marcel Proust, *Correspondance*, vol. 19, p. 575. For Douglas Alden, "Proust demanded satisfaction. Such impetuosity is not surprising in a '*nerveux*,' nor is this dramatic gesture astonishing in a young man, who, at this time, took feudal society seriously. Proust rose to the occasion, demonstrating unusual calmness."

Douglas Alden, "Marcel Proust's Duels," *Modern Language Notes*, February 1938, p. 105. On dueling, see Stefan Geifes, "Le duel à l'époque de l'affaire Dreyfus," in *L'Affaire Dreyfus et le tournant du siècle* (Paris: Musée d'histoire contemporaine-BDIC, 1994).

29. *Correspondance de Marcel Proust*, vol. 19, p. 75. This letter was dated January 15, 1920. The duel with Pierre Weber took place on February 6, 1897. Mme Arman de Caillavet wrote to Proust: "I hug you for your bravery and hope you return safe and sound from this adventure. I wish the monster had suffered some harm, but it's already very nice that you attacked him." *Correspondance de Marcel Proust*, vol. 2, p. 174. Léon Daudet, who made no secret of his anti-Semitism, wrote this of Proust: "I am not surprised that he is always tired. I know of no one more troubled by the psychological and somatic mystery of the past . . . which does not prevent him from taking hold of himself on occasion and showing energy." *Correspondance de Marcel Proust*, vol. 19, p. 75. Daudet added: "he was very brave and defended his friends." *Paris vécu, rive droite* (Paris: Gallimard, 1929), p. 1016.

30. *Correspondance de Marcel Proust*, vol. 21, p. 352. This letter is dated July 16, 1922.

31. *L'Aurore*, October 14, 1912.

32. *L'Intransigeant*, October 15, 1912.

33. *Le Temps*, October 15, 1912. From *Le Petits Parisien*, October 15, 1912: "M. Blum attacked very vigorously. M. Weber broke very much in line. At times, the adversaries seemed to score hits. M. Blum tried to strike his opponent off balance, and at moments both attacked simultaneously. . . . The second round was even more spirited. . . . M. Blum charged his adversary, who attempted several stops and scratched his thigh. . . . Ultimately, he managed to catch the blade and aim at the chest. The thrust hit M. Weber in the sternum and forced him back. . . . The surgeons hastened to the wounded man. The tip had stopped on the last rib, grazing the intercostal nerve on the way."

34. *L'Ouest-Eclair*, October 15, 1912.

35. Birnbaum, *Anti-Semitism in France*, pp. 230 ff.

Chapter 2. The Dreyfus Affair

1. Léon Blum, "Souvenirs sur l'Affaire," in *L'oeuvre de Léon Blum, 1937–1940* (Paris: Albin Michel, 1965), p. 517.

2. Ibid., pp. 520–521.

3. Ibid., p. 520.

4. A. B. Jackson, *La Revue Blanche, 1889–1903* (Paris: Minard, 1960), p. 115. For Jackson, p. 6, "the *Revue Blanche* was something quite different from a Parisian literary magazine. It was also the organ of Jewish culture." A similar view is expressed in William Logue, *Léon Blum: The Formative Years, 1872–1914* (De Kalb: Northern Illinois University Press, 1973), p. 44.

5. André Gide, *Journal*, January 24, 1914 (Paris: Gallimard/ Pléiade, 1999), vol. 1, pp. 762–763. On rereading this text after World War II, Gide wrote: "I am truly grateful to him for not holding against me some rather harsh passages in my *Diary* on the subject of Jews and himself (which, moreover, I cannot renounce because I continue to believe that they are quite correct). He ignored them and never spoke to me about them. Like anyone else, he of course has his faults, and his strike me as quite specifically Jewish faults. But his qualities, even (or especially) those that I believe to be specifically Jewish, outweigh them. He remains for me an admirable representative of both Semitism and humanity, just as in his official and political relations with foreigners he was an excellent representative of France (nationalists to the contrary notwithstanding), to our country's honor." *Gide et Blum: Correspondance, 1890–1950*, expanded edition, edited by Pierre Lachasse (Paris: PUL, 2011), p. 200.

6. Faguet quoted in "Léon Blum avant Léon Blum: Les années littéraires, 1892–1914," *Cahiers Léon Blum*, nos. 23–25, 1988, p. 200.

7. Léon Daudet, *Au temps de Judas* (Paris: Grasset, 1933), p. 111.

8. Lisa Leff, *Sacred Bonds of Solidarity* (Palo Alto: Stanford University Press, 2006).

9. Ibid., p. 518.

10. "Lettre ouverte à M Trarieux," quoted in Nelly Wilson, *Bernard Lazare* (Paris: Albin Michel, 1985), p. 218.

11. Blum, "Souvenirs sur l'Affaire," p. 518.

12. Ibid., p. 535.

13. Cf. Venita Datta, "The Dreyfus Affair and Anti-Semitism: Jewish Identity at *La revue blanche*," *Historical Reflections/Réflexions historiques*, vol. 21, no. 1, 1995, p. 112.

14. One particular ill-disposed critic maintained that "the natural reaction of a sensitive and courageous man like M. Blum, a verbally courageous man, was to declare frankly and forthrightly that he was an Israélite and to reflect on the character of his religion and race—reflections that he would probably never have undertaken had it not been for the error of a military tribunal." Marcel Thiébaut, *En lisant M. Léon Blum* (Paris: Gallimard, 1937), p. 65.

15. Blum, "Souvenirs sur l'Affaire," p. 523.

16. Léon Blum, "Les élections de 1902." The manuscript for this article is in Archives Nationales (French National Archives), Paris (hereinafter cited as AN), 570 AP/3, file 1BL5Dr4. It was published in *L'oeuvre de Léon Blum, 1891–1905*.

17. Blum, "Nouvelles conversations de Goethe avec Eckermann," in *L'oeuvre de Léon Blum, 1891–1905*, pp. 220, 223. In 1903, when introducing Barrès's *Au Service de l'Allemagne*, Blum seems by contrast to have taken his inspiration from Renan-style nationalism, again stressing the contradiction in which Barrès is caught: "By depicting an Alsatian who will not succumb to German culture and domination, M. Barrès implicitly denies any importance to the ethnic element in the formation of modern nationalities. And with that one whole aspect of the nationalist theory collapses. . . . If the Alsatian Ehrmann's heart remains French, it is because a nation is not a homogeneous ethnic formation but an abstract composite of ideas, political notions, and moral concepts." Léon Blum, "En lisant," in *L'oeuvre de Léon Blum, 1891–1905*, pp. 80–81. See Emilien Carassus, "Maurice Barrès et Léon Blum," *Cahiers Léon Blum*, no. 23, 1988, p. 46. Scott Lerner, "Against Ideological Determinism: Blum and Barrès," *Contemporary French Civilization*, winter 2003, no. 1, pp. 58–60.

18. *Gide et Blum: Correspondance, 1890–1950*, p. 80. Gide even-

tually returned Blum's note: "The latest news of the Dreyfus-Ester[hazy] Affair, etc. is overwhelming. I did not sign the Scheurer-Kestner petition at the time of the first Zola letter because it displeased me, as a Protestant, to ally myself with other Protestants. I was afraid that a Jewish or Protestant name no longer meant anything beyond signifying a denomination. Zola's attitude has now become so tragic and beautiful, and the conduct of the 'students' toward him so scandalous, that if there is still time for either this demonstration or another one, I willingly give my name, unknown though it may be" (p. 77).

19. Léon Blum, "Un juriste," in *L'oeuvre de Léon Blum, 1891–1905*, pp. 343, 347, 348.

20. Léon Blum, "Les lois scélérates," in *L'oeuvre de Léon Blum, 1891–1905*, pp. 372–373.

21. Léon Blum, "Nouvelles conversations de Goethe avec Eckermann," in *L'oeuvre de Léon Blum, 1891–1905*, pp. 263–264. This article was reprinted in May 1909.

22. Ibid., p. 266.

23. Ibid., p. 265.

24. Ibid., p. 262.

25. Pierre Birnbaum, *The Anti-Semitic Moment: A Tour of France in 1898* (New York: Hill and Wang, 2003).

26. The allusion is to the Saint Bartholomew's Day massacre of French Protestants that took place in 1572, during the Wars of Religion.

27. Blum, "Nouvelles conversations de Goethe avec Eckermann," in *L'oeuvre de Léon Blum, 1891–1905*, p. 262.

28. Similarly, in 1927, Blum believed that it was "the honor of the proletariat of this country to rise up against injustice . . . to fight for Sacco and Vanzetti as they fought for Dreyfus." *Le Populaire*, September 19, 1927.

29. Blum, *Souvenirs sur l'Affaire*, pp. 520–521. See Baruch Hagani, "M. Léon Blum et l'Affaire Dreyfus," *Cahiers juifs*, June 1936, p. 527.

30. Julien Benda, *La jeunesse d'un clerc* (Paris: Gallimard, 1936), p. 43.

31. André Spire, *Souvenirs à bâtons rompus* (Paris: Albin Michel, 1962), p. 52.

32. Pierre Birnbaum, "La citoyenneté en péril: Les juifs entre intégration et résistance," in Pierre Birnbaum, *La France de l'Affaire Dreyfus* (Paris: Gallimard, 1994), pp. 521 ff. In somewhat contradictory fashion, Wladimir Rabi, after criticizing Hannah Arendt, noted that it was rather "unconditional confidence in France" that accounted for the reserve of French Jews, but then went on to cite André Spire, Émile Durkheim, Paul Grunebaum-Ballin, and Léon Blum: "However, among all [of these Jews], even the most alienated, there was something like a resurgence of an old spirit of solidarity in response to the common ordeal, even if they never discussed it." Wladimir Rabi, "Ecrivains juifs face à l'affaire Dreyfus," in *Les écrivains et l'affaire Dreyfus*, ed. Géraldi Leroy (Paris: PUF, 1983), p. 24.

33. Michael Marrus, *The Politics of Assimilation: A Study of the French Jewish Community at the Time of the Dreyfus Affair* (Oxford: Clarendon Press, 1971).

34. The two quotes from Victor Basch are taken from Nicole Racine, "Ecrivains juifs face à l'affaire Dreyfus," in *Les écrivains et l'affaire Dreyfus*, ed. Géraldi Leroy (Paris: PUF, 1983), p. 24. A little later, in January 1936, Albert Thibaudet wrote that "the three manifestos of intellectuals in October reminded many of us of the days of the Dreyfus Affair. It would not be surprising, moreover, if the Republic had a Dreyfus Affair every thirty years or so, that is, every generation. I wonder if we will see the same thing in 1970 and 2000." See *Réflexions sur la politique*, ed. Antoine Compagnon (Paris: Robert Laffont, 2007), p. 586.

35. Blum, "Souvenirs sur l'Affaire," p. 535.

Chapter 3. On Love

1. Léon Blum, "Declamatio suasoria," in *Cahiers Leon Blum*, "Léon Blum avant Léon Blum, Les années litteraires," nos. 23–25, 1988, p. 99.

2. "Ceci et cela," in *Cahiers Leon Blum*, "Léon Blum avant Léon Blum, Les années litteraires," nos. 23–25, 1988, pp. 103–104.

3. *Correspondance de Marcel Proust*, vol. 6, pp. 136, 138, 149, 286–297, vol. 16, pp. 401–402, vol. 18, pp. 266, 284, vol. 19, pp. xii, 346, 485.

4. Marcel Proust, *Jean Santeuil* (Paris: Gallimard, 2001), pp. 718–719.

5. Michel Crouzet, "'Le Contre Stendhal' de Proust ou cristallisation stendhalienne et cristallisation proustienne," *Stendhal Club*, July 1993, pp. 315–316. Crouzet adds (p. 318) that "there is adulation of Stendhal in Proust, with many tips of the hat." On Stendhalian reminiscences in Proust see also David Backus, "Marcel Proust stendhalien," *Stendhal Club*, April 15, 1982.

6. Voir Pierrette Neaud, "L'«esprit Revue Blanche» et Léon Blum avant Stendhal et le Beylisme," in *Le temps du Stendhal-Club*, ed. Philippe Berthier and Gérald Rannaud (Toulouse: Presses universitaires du Mirail, 1994), p. 128. In the same volume see also Thierry Gouin, "Stendhal, Barrès et moi," pp. 104 ff. On the relation of Proust to Barrès, see Marie Miguet, "Proust et Barrès," *Barrès: Une tradition dans la modernité* (Paris: Champion, 1991); Hidehiko Yuzawa, "Barrès et Proust: Deux usages de la mémoire," in *Proust sans frontières*, ed. Bernard Brun, Masafumi Oguro, and Kazuyoshi Yoshikawa (Caen: Minard, 2009).

7. Léon Blum, *Stendhal et le beylisme* (Paris: Albin Michel, 1947), pp. 3–4.

8. Victor Del Litto, "Stendhal chez Blum," *Stendhal Club*, October 1991, p. 60.

9. Pierre-Louis Rey, "Léon Blum, Stendhal et le Beylisme," in *Le temps du Stendhal-Club*, ed. Philippe Berthier and Gérald Rannaud, p. 194.

10. Jean-Thomas Nordmann argues that Blum's stories include "introspective presentations of some amorous intrigue," a literary device that appealed to Stendhal, whose heroes deliver "soliloquies." Nordmann, "Le Stendhal de Léon Blum," *Stendhal Club*, October 1992, p. 26.

11. Blum, *Stendhal et le beylisme*, pp. 17, 25.

12. Ibid., pp. 21, 32.

13. Ibid., p. 58.

14. See the remarkable work of Manuel Brussaly, *The Political Ideas of Stendhal* (New York: Russell and Russell, 1933).

15. Blum wrote that Stendhal "never owned anything but his clothes, his papers, and a few books." Blum, *Stendhal et le beylisme*, p. 64.

16. Greilsammer, *Blum*, p. 39.

17. Ibid., p. 20.

18. Ibid., p. 161.

19. Siegfried Van Praag, "Marcel Proust, témoin du judaïsme déjudaisé," *Revue Juive de Genève*, nos. 48, 50; Antoine Compagnon, "Le narrateur en procès," *Bulletin Marcel Proust*, 1998, no. 48. See also the fine thesis of Yuji Murakami, in *L'Affaire Dreyfus dans l'oeuvre de Proust* (Paris: Université Paris-Sorbonne, 2012).

20. Blum's unpublished stories and handwritten notes can be found in the Archives Nationales, AN 570/1. Here is a sample: "Valmont deserves better. I am not ashamed that I feel some sympathy for him. . . . A comparison with Don Juan, which could be pushed quite some way, would no doubt prove to Valmont's advantage. He seduced, compromised, and ruined every woman who crossed his path. But what women he met! An imaginary rake and braggart who awaited nothing other than a woman capable of feeling love! . . . The men who have given the most precise descriptions of methods of seductions are, as we know for sure in the case of Stendhal and as is likely in the case of Laclos, men who did not have much success with women. They desired them, displeased them, or allowed them to escape because they lacked wantonness, candor, or audacity, as men who reason too much generally do. . . . It would have been more profitable to act. . . . Those who calculate too much never win in either love or politics."

21. Léon Blum, *Du mariage* (Paris: Albin Michel, 1907), p. 23.

22. Ibid., p. 61.

23. Ibid., p. 65.

24. Ibid., p. 219.

25. Ibid., p. 79.

26. *La Croix des Alpes-Maritimes*, July 7, 1907; *La Libre Parole*, February 8, 1909; *Le Peuple Français*, February 19, 1909; *Jaune*, Feb-

ruary 24, 1909. For all press reviews, see AN, Fondation Nationale des Sciences Politiques, 570 AP/1, files 1/3L3Dr4 and 1NL4Dr2. For Georges Suarez, Blum was now "Beelzebub," the embodiment of all "the vices of bourgeois society"; Suarez, *Nos saigneurs et maîtres* (Paris: Editions de France, 1937), pp. 11–13. Apostrophizing Blum, Jean-Charles Legrand wrote that his book "teaches our wives and daughters to submit to your rutting friends, who lurk behind its covers"; Legrand, *Paroles vivantes* (Paris: Editions Baudinière, 1941), p. 185.

27. *L'Action Française*, April 19, 1937. *Gringoire* saw Blum as a "disciple of the Marquis de Sade"; July 2, 1937.

28. André Gide, *Corydon* (Paris: Gallimard, 1925), p. 115.

29. *Au Pilori*, October 4, 1940.

30. Comte Armand de Puységur, *Les maquereaux légitimes* (Paris, 1938), p. 142.

31. Blum, *Du mariage*, p. 92.

32. APP, BA 1978. According to one police report, "Léon Blum's mistress is the artist Régina Casier." Another report in the same file states that "beautiful Olga" was his mistress.

33. Ilan Greilsammer constructs his biography of Blum around the respective roles of each of his three wives.

34. Blum's letter to Gide, dated November 7, 1895, in *Gide et Blum: Correspondance*, pp. 50–52.

35. AN 570 AP/30, file 5BL2Dr3.

36. Birnbaum, *The Jews of the Republic* (Stanford: Stanford University Press, 1996), chap. 7.

37. Constance Coline, *Le matin vu du soir: De la Belle Epoque aux Années Folles* (Paris: Editions Anthropos, 1980), chap. 12.1. This remarkable work by a young Jewish woman whose life spanned the twentieth century is a good source of detailed information about turn-of-the-century Jewish society. See also Greilsammer, *Blum*, pp. 96–98.

38. AN 570 AP/1, file 1/3L2Dr3.

39. Constance Coline wrote that "things went well in immorality and lying. . . . Did Léon betray Thérèse? Very likely. He liked women and above all loved to be loved. So upright in his

public life, this man, who never deviated an inch from the route he set for himself, was astonishingly self-indulgent in his love life." *Le matin vu du soir*, pp. 229–230. Elsewhere she wrote: "It is odd to think that this apostle of sexual and emotional freedom . . . married three times, each time to a jealous and possessive woman, and that his marriages were extraordinarily conventional, as he lavished care and attention on his wife whenever he violated the marriage contract." (p. 90)

40. Greilsammer, *Blum*, p. 195.

41. Coline, *Le matin vu du soir*, p. 225.

42. Ibid., p. 227.

43. Moscow Archives, inventory 4, file 46, document 124.

44. Ibid.

45. Ibid., document 212.

46. Ibid., document 5.

47. Ibid., document 69.

48. Ibid., documents 6–7. Letter dated August 16, 1914. Some of these letters are reproduced in Serge Berstein, *Léon Blum*, pp. 155 ff.

49. Moscow Archives, inventory 4, file 46, document 55.

50. Ibid.

51. Ibid., document 318.

52. Ibid., document 303.

53. Ibid., letter dated November 21, 1914.

54. Ibid., document 50.

55. Ibid., documents 63–64.

56. Ibid., document 76; Moscow Archives, inventory 4, file 29, document 128.

57. Moscow Archives, inventory 4, file 46, document 68.

58. Ibid., documents 8–10.

59. Ibid., inventory 4, file 48.

60. Ibid., inventory 4, file 29.

61. Ibid., inventory 4, file 48.

62. Ibid., dated August 31, 1920. Thérèse also revealed her jealousy: "I confess I would like to have this night with you over

again. I had you all to myself, truly to myself." Ibid., inventory 4, file 46, August 1920, document 257.

63. Ibid., inventory 4, file 29, documents 28–29. Letter of June 23, 1921.

64. Ibid., inventory 4, file 39.

65. Ibid., inventory 4, file 46, document 45. Letter of October 23, 1925.

66. Ibid., inventory 4, file 32, document 2.

67. Ibid., inventory 4, file 33, document 36.

68. Ibid., inventory 4, file 29, document 36.

69. Ibid., inventory 4, file 31. Letter of October 2, 1923.

70. Ibid., inventory 4, file 38.

71. Ibid., inventory 4, file 31, documents 3–4. Letter of July 30, 1925. With a few minor differences, this letter can also be found in Berstein, *Léon Blum*, pp. 260–261.

72. Moscow Archives, inventory 4, file 48, document 294. Letter of March 17, 1929.

73. Ibid., inventory 4, file 48, document 94. Letter of April 13, 1929.

74. Ibid., inventory 4, file 48, document 101. On April 14, from Narbonne, he wrote to Thérèse: "My beloved! I love you, I love you." Ibid., document 96.

75. Ibid., document 51. Letter of March 2, 1929.

76. Ibid., inventory 4, file 48, document 75. Letter of March 5, 1929.

77. Ibid., document 86. Letter of March 26, 1929.

78. Ibid., document 48.

79. Ibid., inventory 4, file 39.

80. AN 570 AP/7, file 1BL11Dr2.

81. Moscow Archives, inventory 4, file 46, document 123.

82. Ibid., document 222.

83. Ibid., document 300.

84. Ibid., document 337.

85. Ibid., document 353. See also document 264.

86. Greilsammer, *Blum*, p. 310.

87. Léon Blum, *Lettres de Buchenwald,* ed. Ilan Greilsammer (Paris: Gallimard, 2003).

Chapter 4. The Heir of Jaurès

1. Louis Lévy, *Comment ils sont devenus socialistes* (Paris: Editions du Populaire, 1932), p. 18.

2. Blum, "Nouvelles conversations de Goethe avec Eckermann," in *L'oeuvre de Léon Blum, 1891–1905,* pp. 266–267.

3. Léon Blum, review of Maurice Donnay's play "Le retour de Jérusalem," in *L'oeuvre de Léon Blum, 1891–1905,* p. 209. For Annie Kriegel, "Léon Blum discovered within himself, intact, an accumulated reserve of ancient tastes, feelings, and values, a reserve that fueled his unwavering ethical concerns and shaped something in him reminiscent of the 'Just' in Hebraic tradition." Annie Kriegel, *Aux origines du communisme français* (Paris: Flammarion/Champ, 1969), p. 360.

4. AN 570 AP/26, file 4BL8Dr2.

5. Léon Blum, "Première et dernière rencontres," in *L'oeuvre de Léon Blum, 1936–1940,* pp. 479–480.

6. Léon Blum, "Souvenirs sur l'Affaire," p. 575.

7. Quoted in Jean Lacouture, *Léon Blum,* pp. 84–85.

8. Philip Kolb, "Proust's Portrait of Jean Jaurès in *Jean Santeuil,*" *French Studies,* October 1961.

9. Marcel Fournier, *Emile Durkheim, 1858–1917* (Paris: Fayard, 2007), pp. 579, 643.

10. These letters, from the "Moscow Archives," are discussed in Berstein, *Léon Blum,* pp. 82 ff. See also Greilsammer, *Blum,* pp. 140 ff.

11. "Jean Jaurès, les socialistes et l'Affaire Dreyfus," *Jean Jaurès Cahiers trimestriels,* 1995, 10–12.

12. Quoted in Marc Sadoun, *De la démocratie française: Essai sur le socialisme* (Paris: Gallimard, 1993), p. 33. See Aaron Noland, "Individualism in Jean Jaurès' Socialist Thought," *Journal of the History of Ideas,* vol. 22, 1961, pp. 75 ff.

13. Léon Blum, "L'idée d'une biographie de Jaurès," *L'oeuvre de Léon Blum, 1914–1928,* p. 5.

14. Jean Jaurès, "Le socialisme de la Révolution française," quoted in Gilles Candar, "Jean Jaurès et le réformisme," *Histoire@ Politique*, January–April 2011, no. 13, p. 2.

15. Jean Jaurès, *L'esprit du socialisme* (Paris: Gonthier, 1964), p. 21.

16. Jean Jaurès, *L'armée nouvelle* (Paris: Fayard, 2012), p. 407.

17. Jean Jaurès, *Études socialistes* (Geneva: Slatkine, 1979), pp. xlv, lxiii.

18. Bruno Antonini, *État et socialisme chez Jean Jaurès* (Paris: L'Harmattan, 2008), pp. 164 ff. With this in mind, it is easier to understand the relation between Jaurès and the reformism of Paul Brousse and his followers, who were willing to participate in electoral politics. Socialists sometimes supported the reformists and even participated in reformist coalitions.

19. Jaurès, *L'armée nouvelle*, p. 380.

20. Quoted in Alain Bergounioux and Gérard Grunberg, *Le long remords du pouvoir: Le Parti socialiste français, 1905–1992* (Paris: Fayard, 1992), p. 24.

21. Although Jaurès accepted the conclusions of the 1904 Amsterdam Congress of the Socialist International, which condemned all collaboration with bourgeois governments and defended the Marxist revolutionary ideal against Édouard Bernstein, he supported the incrementalist, revisionist approach of the French government in its quest for social compromise. In Germany, orthodox Marxists vigorously opposed such revisionism, and even stronger opposition would emerge in France at a somewhat later date.

22. Blum, "Nouvelles conversations de Goethe avec Eckermann," in *L'oeuvre de Léon Blum, 1891–1905*, pp. 289–290.

23. Robert Smith, "L'atmosphère politique à l'École normale supérieure à la fin du XIXè siècle," *Revue d'histoire moderne et contemporaine*, April 1973, pp. 257, 264. See also Madeleine Rebérioux, "Jaurès et Blum," *Cahiers Léon Blum*, no. 11.

24. Christophe Charle maintains that "the overrepresentation of Jews was the most distinctive religious characteristic of the socialist *normaliens*." Charle, "Les Normaliens et le socialisme

NOTES TO PAGES 60–66

(1867–1914)," in *Jaurès et les intellectuels,* ed. Madeleine Rebérioux and Gilles Candar (Paris: Les Editions de l'Atelier, 1994), p. 156.

25. Emmanuel Jousse, "La tentation révisionniste et la construction d'un réformisme français," *Histoire@Politique: Politique, culture, société,* January–April 2011, p. 11; Moscow Archives, inventory 1, file 335. See also long letters from Blum to Herr about Jaurès and *L'Humanité,* AN 570 AP/3, file 1BL5Dr3.

26. Léon Blum, "Réflexion sur le congrès socialiste," *La Revue Blanche,* no. 158, January 1, 1900.

27. Blum, "Débats intérieurs," in *L'oeuvre de Léon Blum, 1914–1928,* p. 123.

28. Blum, "Idée d'une biographie de Jaurès," in *L'oeuvre de Léon Blum, 1914–1928,* pp. 12, 17, 19.

29. Blum, "Commentaires sur le programme d'action du parti socialiste," in *L'oeuvre de Léon Blum, 1914–1928,* p. 111.

30. *L'Humanité,* November 15, 1918, quoted in Joel Colton, *Léon Blum* (Paris: Fayard, 1967), p. 56.

31. Blum, "Débats intérieurs," in *L'oeuvre de Léon Blum, 1914–1928,* pp. 133–135.

32. Annie Kriegel, *Le Congrès de Tours* (Paris: Julliard/Archives, 1964).

33. *Le Congrès de Tours,* critical edition by Jean Charles et al. (Paris: Editions sociales, 1980), pp. 112 ff.

34. Ibid., pp. 151 ff.

35. Ibid., pp. 217–218.

36. Ibid., p. 358.

37. Blum, "Le Congrès de Tours," in *L'oeuvre de Léon Blum, 1914–1928,* pp. 142–144.

38. Ibid., p. 151.

39. Annie Kriegel argues that "it bears emphasizing that Blum in 1920 was not a French Bernstein: the leader of the opposition to the Third International intended to maintain socialism as a revolutionary enterprise." Kriegel, *Aux origines du communisme français,* p. 364.

40. Blum, "Le congrès de Tours," p. 154.

41. Ibid.

42. Ibid., p. 159.

43. *Le Congrès de Tours*, ed. Jean Charles et al., pp. 435–436.

44. Ibid., p. 443. By contrast, Frossard lavishly praised "the admirable effort" of "our friend Léon Blum" and insisted on "his talent, his vast culture, and his tireless effort." Ibid., pp. 482, 520.

45. Ibid., p. 550.

46. Léon Blum, "Controverse sur la dictature," in *L'oeuvre de Léon Blum, 1914–1928*, p. 251.

47. Léon Blum, "L'idéal socialiste," in *L'oeuvre de Léon Blum, 1914–1928*, p. 360.

48. Léon Blum, "Bolchévisme et socialisme," article of March 1927, in *L'oeuvre de Léon Blum, 1914–1928*, pp. 453, 460.

49. Unpublished lecture, AN 570 AP/6, file 1BL10Dr3.

50. Avner Ben-Amos, "La 'panthéonisation' de Jean Jaurès: Rituel et politique pendant la IIIè République," *Terrain*, no. 15, October 1990. In 1937, Blum delivered another memorial speech for Jaurès in front of the Panthéon. *Le Populaire*, August 1, 1937. See also the manuscript of his speech at the Panthéon on July 31, 1947, AN 570 AP/26.

51. Léon Blum, unpublished lecture, AN 570 AP/6, file 1BL10Dr3.

52. Léon Blum, "Cours sur Jaurès," AN 570 AP/6, file 1BL 10Dr2.

53. Léon Blum, "Jean Jaurès," lecture delivered on February 16, 1933, at the Théâtre des Ambassadeurs, in *Cahiers Léon Blum*, no. 11, p. 79.

54. Ibid., p. 69.

55. Imprisoned at Portalet by Vichy in 1941, Blum wrote *À l'échelle humaine*, which is full of references to Jaurès: see, e.g, *L'oeuvre de Léon Blum, 1940–1945*, pp. 453, 454, 466, 484. Later, at Buchenwald in 1944, he asked: "What does it mean to be faithful to Jaurès's thought today?" And in the same year: "We will not tolerate attacks on Jaurès's imperishable work." AN 570 AP/21.

56. Fraser and Natanson, *Léon Blum: Man and Statesman*, p. 77.

57. In 1946, being once again close to achieving political power, Blum remarked: "I am old and will not see the Promised

Land. I will not see the perfect union of nations in justice and peace." Quoted in Greilsammer, *Blum*, p. 522. On returning to Paris in 1946, Blum again repeatedly invoked the spirit of Jaurès. See, for example, *Le Populaire*, May 22, July 31, August 9 and 14, 1945.

Chapter 5. In Service of the State

1. Even after becoming involved in politics, Blum remained attached to the Council of State—indeed, so attached that after his election as deputy he wrote to the Minister of Justice asking if he could remain because he could not "resign" himself to leaving. His request was denied. See Dominique Chagnollaud, *Le premier des ordres, les hauts fonctionnaires XVIIIe–XXe siècles* (Paris: Fayard, 1991), p. 361.

2. Greilsammer, *Blum*, p. 526, argues that Blum should not be categorized as a state Jew because he did not revere the Republic as much as he did literature and socialism. But one can also see him as a state Jew respectful of the republican order yet also deeply concerned by questions of social justice to which state action could at best provide only partial answers.

3. Blum, "Nouvelles conversations de Goethe avec Eckermann," in *L'oeuvre de Léon Blum, 1891–1905*, p. 220.

4. Blum, *L'oeuvre de Léon Blum, 1934–1937*, p. 273.

5. Ibid., p. 473.

6. Pierre Birnbaum, "La conception durkheimienne de l'État," *Revue française de sociologie* 17, 1976.

7. Quoted in Rolande Trempé, "Jaurès, l'État, la réforme et la révolution, Jaurès et l'État," *Cahiers Jean Jaurès*, October–December 1998, p. 8.

8. Léon Blum, "À l'échelle humaine," in *L'oeuvre de Léon Blum, 1940–1945*, p. 470.

9. *Le Populaire*, June 15, 1947; *L'oeuvre de Léon Blum, 1945–1947*, p. 57. See Leo Hamon, "État, socialisme et pouvoir dans l'oeuvre de Léon Blum," *Cahiers Léon Blum*, no. 11. Blum understood "the significance of the state," according to Jacques Marchal, "Léon Blum et l'exercice du pouvoir," in *Léon Blum et l'État* (Paris:

Centre National de la Recherche Scientifique, CNRS), June 1973, p. 71.

10. Léon Blum, "Exercice et conquête du pouvoir," in *L'oeuvre de Léon Blum, 1945–1947*, pp. 435–436.

11. Vincent Le Grand, *Léon Blum (1872–1950): Gouverner la République* (Paris: L.G.D.J., 2008), p. 7.

12. Ibid., pp. 484 ff. Jérôme Michel, *Blum, un juriste en politique* (Paris: Michalon, 2008), p. 63, also argues that Blum "implicitly" adopted Duguit's doctrine. By contrast, Hugo-Bernard Pouillaude denies in a recent article that Duguit exerted any direct influence on Blum, although he does point out that both defended public service. Pouillaude believes that Blum was influenced more by Benoît Malon and Paul Brousse. Pouillaude, "Itinéraires croisés des oeuvres de Léon Blum et de Léon Duguit," *Revue française de droit administratif*, 2013, no. 1, p. 186. Damien Fallon, "Léon Blum et la fonction administrative," *Revue française de droit administratif*, 2013, no. 1, pp. 162 ff, argues that Blum was influenced more by Hauriou's theory of public authority.

13. Ibid., pp. 513–514.

14. Ibid.

15. Aude Zaradny, "Léon Blum, un socialiste au Conseil d'Etat," *Revue française de droit administratif*, 2013, no. 1, p. 3.

16. Georges Cahen-Salvador, "De quelques personnalités qui ont illustré le Conseil d'Etat au XIXè siècle," in *Le Conseil d'État: Livre jubilaire publié pour commémorer son cent cinquantième anniversaire* (Paris: Sirey, 1952), p. 293. On Blum's work for the Council of State, see Pierre Juvigny, "Un grand commissaire du gouvernement: Léon Blum," in *Le Conseil d'État: Livre jubilaire*, and, more recently, Alain Chatriot, "Léon Blum et le Conseil d'État," in *Cahiers Léon Blum*, no. 35, spring 2006, p. 12.

17. Blum, "La réforme gouvernementale," in *L'oeuvre de Léon Blum, 1914–1928*, p. 513.

18. Ibid., pp. 515, 518.

19. Ibid., pp. 544, 549.

20. In practice, the "waltz" of high civil servants advocated by many socialist militants did not take place; changes were limited.

See Irwin Wall, "Socialists and Bureaucrats: The Blum Government and the French Administration, 1936–1937," *International Review of Social History*, 1974, vol. 19, p. 332.

21. Blum, "La réforme gouvernementale," in *L'oeuvre de Léon Blum, 1914–1928*, p. 574.

22. Birnbaum, *The Jews of the Republic*, chap. 18.

23. Quoted in Lacouture, *Léon Blum*, p. 206.

24. See, for example, his speeches to the Chamber of Deputies on November 26, 1931, and October 28, 1932. He also spoke out frequently against Hitler and the danger of racism. See, for example, his speech at the Salle Wagram, March 2, 1933. *Le Populaire*, March 3, 1933.

25. Paul Jankowski, *Cette vilaine affaire Stavisky: Histoire d'un scandale politique* (Paris: Fayard, 2000).

26. Quoted in Serge Berstein, *Le 6 février 1934* (Paris: Archives, 1975), p. 143.

27. Pierre Pellissier, *6 février 1934: La République en flammes* (Paris: Perrin, 2000), p. 209.

28. On February 6, 1946, Blum revisited the events of 1934: "Yes, on the faces of many deputies, the cowardly terror of Vichy was written in advance. Yes, the future men of Vichy were there. On the whole, however, the Chamber of February 6 was in no way the National Assembly of Vichy." *Le Populaire*, February 6, 1946.

29. Pellissier, *6 février 1934: La République en flammes*, p. 209.

30. Blum, "Le problème du pouvoir et le fascisme," in *L'oeuvre de Léon Blum, 1936–1947*, p. 195.

31. Jean-François Biard, "Le débat sur le régime intermédiaire et le plan, juillet 1933–juillet 1934," *Cahiers Léon Blum*, 1984, no. 15.

32. Blum, "Exercice et conquête du pouvoir," in *L'oeuvre de Léon Blum, 1945–1947*, p. 432.

33. Ibid., p. 436.

Chapter 6. The Attack

1. Cédric Gruat, "1936: L'agression filmée de Léon Blum," *Arkheia*, nos. 17–18.

2. *Le Populaire*, February 14, 1936.

3. *Le Matin,* February 14, 1936.

4. Léon Blum, speech at Narbonne, October 25, 1936, AN 570 AP/13, file 2BL3Dr3.

5. Montel, a close friend, had previously represented Blum's former district as a Socialist deputy and was in charge of Socialist Party activities in the region. Montel responded the next day: "I cannot accept responsibility for what happens, and I would be ashamed if we did not carry out the promised reprisals. Despite your telegram, which was meant to reassure and calm, I cannot promise what you are asking for." AN F/7/13964.

6. *Le Populaire,* February 14, 1936. See also *Le Petit Parisien,* February 14, 1936.

7. Moscow Archives, inventory 1, file 335, documents 3–4.

8. Ibid., documents 5–6.

9. Ibid., inventory 2, file 666, documents 14–15.

10. *Le Petit Bleu,* February 14, 1936.

11. *L'Action Française,* February 14, 1936. See also *Le Jour,* February 14, 1936. Meanwhile, Henri de Kerillis saw Blum as a "theorist of violence, a provocateur," but "deplored" the attack on a defenseless man. *L'Echo de Paris,* February 14, 1936.

12. APP, BA 1862, report of February 15, 1934.

13. Ibid. This is a second police report drafted on the same date, February 15.

14. Ibid., report of February 17, 1936.

15. Ibid., report of February 19, 1936.

16. *Le Populaire,* February 18, 1936.

17. *Vendredi,* February 18, 1936.

18. *L'Action Française,* February 18, 1936.

19. *L'Ami du Peuple,* February 17, 1936.

20. See *Le Charivari,* June 6, 1936, and *Gringoire,* September 14, 1936.

21. *Le Populaire,* November 19, 1938.

22. *La Tribune Juive,* April 3, 1936. A short while later, on April 20, 1936, *L'Univers Israélite* wrote: "We are not concerned here with the political opinions of M. Léon Blum or M. François Coty.

We consider both to be good Frenchmen until proof of the contrary arrives."

23. *L'Univers Israélite*, May 22, 1936.

24. *Samedi*, May 23, 1936.

25. *L'Univers Israélite*, May 8, 1936.

26. *L'Univers Israélite*, June 19, 1936.

27. *La Tribune Juive*, June 12, 1936.

28. In Pierre Renouvin and René Rémond, eds., *Léon Blum, chef de gouvernement* (Paris: FNSP, 1967), p. 146.

29. Letter of February 10, 1934, private archives of Philippe Landau. Similarly, Émile Milhaud wrote to the Grand Rabbi that Blum's politics could only "injure his co-religionists."

30. For *La Tribune Juive*, February 21, 1936, "the socialist leader Léon Blum, the victim of an attack by his political enemies, is not a Jewish militant, and he has chosen to use his dazzling talent and remarkable intelligence in a cause that is not ours. We therefore need not concern ourselves here with this affair, which has the political world in an uproar. . . . As a politician, M. Blum represents a political idea that is not a Jewish idea." Concerning these contrasting reactions, see Birnbaum, *Anti-Semitism in France*, chap. 3.

31. *Le Droit de Vivre*, May 23, 1936.

32. *Naie Presse*, July 14, 1936. This paper repeatedly denounced the "Two Hundred Families," who were alleged to be working to overthrow the Popular Front. See also *Naie Presse*, May 5, 1936, and June 23, 1937.

33. For Jabotinsky, "the Blum episode may become one of the bitterest and most sorrowful phases in the history of Jew-hatred. . . . If it fails, the Jews will pay for it, and one of the few countries where one may still breathe freely will be poisoned for many years with hostility and contempt from both Right and Left." Quoted in Zacariah Shuster, "As Leon Blum Began to Reign," *The Menorah Journal*, October 1936, p. 314.

34. *L'Action Française*, April 21, 1920.

35. Hubert Bourgin, *De Jaurès à Blum* (Paris: Fayard, 1938), p. 498.

36. *L'Action Française*, April 23, 1937.

37. Ibid., April 9, 1935.

38. Léon Daudet, *L'Action Française*, June 1, 1936.

39. Jean Renaud, *Solidarité Française*, December 7, 1935.

40. Maurice Bedel, *Bengali* (Paris: Oeuvres françaises, 1937), p. 108.

41. Marcel Jouhandeau, *Le péril Juif* (Paris: Fernand Sorlot, 1936), p. 12.

42. Marcel Jouhandeau, *Je Suis Partout*, July 30, 1937.

43. *Candide*, October 8, 1936, and April 7, 1938.

44. *Gringoire*, June 5, 1936.

45. Henri Béraud, *Trois ans de colère* (Paris: Editions de France, 1936), p. 150.

46. Bedel, *Bengali*, pp. 116 ff. See also Birnbaum, *Anti-Semitism in France*, chap. 6.

47. *Le Courrier de Narbonne*, August 1, 1935.

48. *L'Indépendant de l'Aube*, March 7, 1936.

49. *L'Action Française*, April 16, 1929.

50. *Je Suis Partout*, January 1, 1935.

51. Maurice Thorez, "Léon Blum tel qu'il est," *L'Internationale Communiste*, no. 2, February 1940. See Annie Kriegel, "Un phénomène de haine fratricide: Léon Blum vu par les communistes," in Kriegel, *Le pain et les roses*, (1968), pp. 392–394. The Sentier was more a district of small Jewish shops and craftsmen, many of whom were immigrants, than a "modern temple of the Golden Calf."

52. *Grande encyclopédie soviétique*, Moscow, vol. 5, 1950, p. 60.

53. *Le Rire*, May 9, 1936.

54. *Les Hommes du Jour*, April 15, 1937, p. 2.

55. *Le Charivari*, June 20, 1936.

56. Quoted in Ralph Schor, *L'antisémitisme en France pendant les années trente* (Paris: Complexe, 1992), p. 174.

57. Laurent Viguier, *Les Juifs à travers Léon Blum: Leur incapacité historique à diriger un État* (1938), p. 8.

58. Henri Béraud, *Popu-Roi*, p. 146.

59. Gustave Téry, "La vie de Monsieur Blum," *L'Action Publique*, 1936, p. 13.

60. Birnbaum, *Les deux maisons*, chap. 4.

Chapter 7. Popular Front!

1. For Louise Elliott Dalby, "the charming and impertinent playboy once known as 'Petit Bob' . . . the rather effeminate dandy with boutonnière, cane and pearl-gray gloves was nevertheless, '*le patron*' to thousands of French workers." Dalby, *Leon Blum* (New York: Thomas Yoseloff, 1963), p. 24.

2. The original of this text can be found in AN 570 AP/12. See also Jean-Michel Gaillard, *Les 40 jours de Blum* (Paris: Perrin 2001), p. 238.

3. Blum was regularly referred to as the *chef* of the left. See, e.g., "Un chef: Léon Blum," *Les Hommes du jour,* May 21, 1936, AN 570 AP/12.

4. Marcel Déat, a rival of Blum's who would later become a collaborator of the Nazis, mocked Blum's distinctions. Blum, he argued, would be forced "to invent the 'occupation of power,' a refinement of the 'exercise' of power, because this time they were resigned to doing nothing. . . . Never had a true revolutionary spirit been so alien to the party." Déat, *Mémoires politiques* (Paris: Denoël, 1989), pp. 279–280.

5. On May 27, Marcel Pivert, an extremist Socialist leader, proclaimed that "Everything is possible!" In response, on May 29, *L'Humanité,* now the Communist Party paper, wrote: "No! Everything is not possible!"

6. AN 570 AP/12, file 2BL2Dr5.

7. Nicolas Roussellier, "Le Front populaire, un régime politique nouveau?" in *Les deux France du Front populaire,* ed. Gilles Morin and Gilles Richard (Paris: L'Harmattan, 2008), pp. 267 ff.

8. Antoine Prost, "Les grèves de juin 1936: Essai d'interprétation," in *Léon Blum, chef de gouvernement,* ed. Pierre Renouvin and René Rémond (Paris: FNSP, 1981), p. 85, and Prost, "Les grèves de mai-juin 1936 revisitées," *Le mouvement social,* July–September 2002. Stéphane Sirot, "La vague de grèves du Front populaire: Des interprétations divergentes et incertaines," in *Les deux France du Front populaire,* ed. Morin and Richard, pp. 51 ff. See also Jacques Kergoat, *La France du Front populaire* (Paris: La Découverte, 2006), chap. 4.

9. Nicolas Roussellier, "La culture économique de Léon

Blum: Entre libéralisme juridique et socialisme," *Histoire@ Politique*, January–April 2012, argues, however, that Blum's economic thinking still bore the stamp of Belle Époque liberalism, which prevented him from implementing a truly interventionist economic policy.

10. Etienne Gout, Pierre Juvigny, and Michel Mousel, "La politique sociale du Front populaire," in *Léon Blum, chef de gouvernement*, ed. Renouvin and Rémond, pp. 245 ff.

11. See, for example, Danielle Tartakowsky, *Le Front populaire: La vie est à nous* (Paris: Découvertes Gallimard, 1996); Jean-Pierre Rioux, *Au bonheur la France* (Paris: Perrin, 2004).

12. Simone Weil, *La condition ouvrière* (Paris: Gallimard, 1951), pp. 168, 229, and 230.

13. Quoted by Jules Moch in his intervention at the Colloque Léon Blum, *Léon Blum, chef de gouvernement*, ed. Renouvin and Rémond, p. 98.

14. Pascal Ory, *La belle illusion: Culture et politique sous le signe du Front populaire* (Paris: Plon, 1994); Julian Jackson, *The Popular Front in France Defending Democracy, 1934–1938* (Cambridge, England: Cambridge University Press, 1988), chap. 4.

15. Léon Blum, "La prison et le procès," in *L'oeuvre de Léon Blum, 1940–1945*, p. 289.

16. Moscow Archives. These postcards are from inventory 4, file 72.

17. Ibid.

18. Timothy Maga, "Closing the Door: The French Government and Refugee Policy, 1933–1939," *French Historical Studies*, spring 1982. See also R. Harouni,"Le débat autour du statut des étrangers," *Le Mouvement social*, July–September 1999, p. 62.

19. Vicky Caron, *Uneasy Asylum: France and the Jewish Refugee Crisis, 1933–1942* (Redwood City: Stanford University Press), 1999.

20. Ralph Schorr, *L'Opinion française et les étrangers en France, 1919–1939* (Paris: Publications de la Sorbonne, 1985).

21. Debate in the Chamber of Deputies, February 19, 1935, *Cahiers Léon Blum*, May 1998, no. 31, p. 75.

22. Léon Blum, speech to the Chamber of Deputies, January 30, 1935, p. 75.

23. Léon Blum, "Contre le racisme," in *Blum: Discours politiques,* ed. Alain Bergounioux (Paris: Imprimerie Nationale, 1997), pp. 211–217. In *Le Populaire* on November 27, 1938, a somewhat different transcript was published: "That is what the Jewish people are victims of. But they are not the only victims—never forget that." For Michael Marrus and Robert Paxton, "Few political leaders denounced the hostility toward immigrants more forcefully than Léon Blum." Marrus and Paxton, *Vichy et les Juifs* (Paris: Calmann-Lévy, 1981), p. 62. At about the same time, the Blum-Violette plan proposed granting French citizenship to Algerian nationals.

24. Emmanuel Naquet, *La Ligue des Droits de l'Homme: Une association politique, 1898–1940,* doctoral thesis, Institut d'études politiques, Paris, 2005, p. 706. See also Max Likin, *Defending Civil Society and the State: The Ligue des Droits de l'Homme in French and European Politics, 1898–1948,* doctoral thesis, Rutgers University, 2004, pp. 189–224.

25. Ellen Perry, *Remembering Dreyfus: The Ligue des Droits de l'Homme and the Making of the Modern French Human Rights Movement,* doctoral thesis, University of North Carolina, 1998, pp. 185–200, argues that "Jews were among the most militant on the Interwar Committee and assumed increased responsibilities in Ligue leadership. (Basch, Kahn, Hadamard, Brunschvicg, Grumbach, Gombault, Kayser, Bloch, Corcos, Veril, Porto-Rice, Blum, Boris, Gougenheim, Milhaud, Raynal, Picard, Ancelle.) Basch was elected the Ligue's first Jewish president in 1926 and Kahn the group's first general secretary in 1932. Grumbach, Hadamard, Gombault and Brunschvicg were powerful presences on the interwar Committee, which the Ligue's enemies, from Right to Left, did not fail to point out."

26. Some writers allege that the Popular Front did not change French policy regarding immigrants. See Rita Thalmann, "L'accueil des émigrés allemands en France de 1933 à la déclaration de guerre," *Emigrés français en Allemagne émigrés allemands en France*

(Paris, 1983), p. 122, and Jean-Claude Bonnet, *Les pouvoirs publics français et l'immigration dans l'entre-deux-guerres* (Lyon: Centre d'histoire économique et sociale de la région lyonnaise, University of Lyon II, 1976). See also Daniel Gordon, "The Back Door of the Nation-State: Expulsions of Foreigners and Continuity in Twentieth-Century France," *Past and Present*, February 2005. By contrast, Vicky Caron emphasizes the more favorable attitude of the Popular Front. Caron, *Uneasy Asylum*, pp. 119–120.

27. Moscow Archives, inventory 2, file 176, and inventory 3, file 37. See also private archives of Marcel Livian, carton 10-1-3, file 47, Office Universitaire de Recherche Socialiste (OURS), as well as the André Blumel archives, 14 APO 4, File Blum, OURS.

28. Livian, *Le Parti socialiste et l'immigration*, p. 116. Patrick Weil, *La France et ses étrangers* (Paris: Calmann-Lévy, 2005), p. 28, argues that "at the base, the bureaucracy seems to have been more influenced by the ambient xenophobia and to have operated somewhat autonomously from the national government, taking zealous repressive measures on its own."

29. Claire Zalc, "Des réfugiés aux indésirables: Les pouvoirs publics français face aux émigrés du IIIè Reich entre 1933 et 1939," in *Constructions des nationalités et immigration dans la France contemporaine*, ed. Eric Guichard and Gérard Noiriel (Paris: Presses de l'École Normale Supérieure, 1997), p. 265. Mary D. Lewis, *Les Frontières de la République* (2010), p. 252.

30. Marc-Olivier Baruch, *Servir l'État français: L'administration en France de 1940 à 1944* (Paris: Fayard, 1997).

31. M. D. Gallagher, "Leon Blum and the Spanish Civil War," *Journal of Contemporary History*, vol. 6, no. 3, 1971, pp. 61–63.

32. In handwritten notes he made at Buchenwald in 1944, Blum discussed his distress over the war in Spain in several places. AN 570 AP/21.

33. *L'oeuvre de Léon Blum, 1934–1937*, p. 388. The next day, September 7, *Le Populaire* ran the following headline on page 1: "Léon Blum magisterially explained the Popular Front government's position on the events in Spain."

34. Colette Audry criticized Blum harshly for abandoning the

Spanish Republicans: "Léon Blum was a delicate soul and . . . was not ashamed of it." Audry, *Léon Blum ou la politique du Juste*, p. 120.

35. Letter dated February 1948, AN 570 AP/23, file 4BL4DR4. Similarly, Vincent Auriol, though favorable to aiding the Spanish government, spoke out against the allegations against Blum, noting that the general staff was not prepared to risk war without English support. "Only a policy of non-intervention by all countries would help or save the Spanish Republic." Unpublished letter to Janot, Blum's wife, AN 570 AP/13, 2BL4Dr1.

36. AN 570 AP/30, file 5BL2DR 3. This letter is dated January 8, 1952.

37. The letter can be found in AN 570 AP/13, file 2BL4Dr2.

38. Blum justified his pacifist policies by saying that he was working toward general disarmament. In May 1930, he wrote: "We want no more war. . . . France should set an example of disarmament." *Le Populaire*, May 15, 1930. See also the articles of May 18 and 19 and June 28, 1930. Following Jaurès, he called for international arbitration to prevent war; *Le Populaire*, January 3 and 18, 1931. In 1931 and 1932, he wrote many articles calling for general disarmament in response to the threat of war from Italy and Germany. He hoped that the Socialist International and the Socialist Parties of Germany and Italy would block the path to war. On February 2 he insisted once more: "Disarmament More Now than Ever." On March 17, 1933, he argued that "there is no reason to fear direct contagion from Hitlerian racism," but called on Socialists to combat nationalist propaganda. On March 31, he denounced Hitlerian racism and the "terror" it aroused. He feared its "cruelty," and on May 20, 1933, following a violent speech by Hitler, he said that "in order to block the route to racist German rearmament, egalitarian disarmament must be achieved." On August 31, 1933, he called on the League of Nations to prevent German rearmament, and on October 1, 1933, he again argued that "the working class is opposed to war." On March 16, 1935, he again expressed hostility to the arms race. In July 1936, as prime minister, he again called on the League of Nations to use "the arms of law"; *Le Populaire*, July 2, 1936. As late as August 1939, Blum de-

clared, "No, war is not inevitable"; *Le Populaire*, August 11, 1939. On September 9, he refused "to repent of any such error. It shows how ardently, how passionately, I wanted peace preserved." He added: "I declare without hesitation, insofar as the enemy allows, our war will be humane. It will be doubly humane because we are fighting for humankind"; *Le Populaire*, September 9, 1939.

39. Georges Vidal, "Le PCF et la défense nationale à l'époque du Front populaire," *Guerres mondiales et conflits contemporains*, 2004, no. 215, p. 61.

40. Annie Kriegel, "Léon Blum et le parti communiste," in *Léon Blum, chef de gouvernement*, ed. Renouvin and Rémond, p. 132.

41. Romain Rolland, *Journal de Vézelay, 1938–1940* (Paris: Bartillat, 2012), p. 140.

42. Moscow Archives, inventory 3, file 37.

43. See all his articles in *Le Populaire* in September 1938 protesting any interference with the territorial integrity of Czechoslovakia.

44. References can be found in Birnbaum, *Anti-Semitism in France*, pp. 268 ff.

Chapter 8. From Vichy to Buchenwald

1. Blum, "Mémoires," in *L'oeuvre de Léon Blum, 1894–1954*, p. 13.

2. This little-known note can be found in AN 570 AP/14, file 2BL5Dr2.

3. "Mémoires," in *L'oeuvre de Léon Blum, 1940–1945*, pp. 60–61.

4. Ibid., pp. 61–62.

5. A police report stated that Blum had joined a group of Jewish lawyers who "are waging a vigorous campaign against the anti-Semitic tendency in the government." APP, BA 1978.

6. "Mémoires," in *L'oeuvre de Léon Blum, 1940–1945*, pp. 83–87, 93. The original manuscript can be found in AN 570 AP/19.

7. Colton, *Léon Blum*, p. 381.

8. This identification card can be found in AN 570 AP/14, file 2BL5Dr2. The same carton also contains Blum's passport along with other personal papers, including his membership card from the Chamber of Deputies and a permit, signed by Daladier, al-

lowing him to travel in the "interior zone" as a member of the Armed Services Committee. Another carton from the postwar era contains another passport, Socialist Party membership cards, and other cards. AN 570 AP/27, file 4BL9Dr2.

9. Blum, in *L'oeuvre de Léon Blum, 1940–1945*, p. 100.

10. Ibid., p. 119.

11. AN 570 AP/19, file 3BL1Dr2.

12. As a police report notes, his own books were taken from his home in late 1940: "They were placed in chests by French packers working under the orders of several German officers and loaded into a truck belonging to the Wehrmacht. The German officers were accompanied by a number of civilians believed to be members of the Gestapo." APP, BA 1978.

13. Quoted in Dominique Missika, *Je vous promets de revenir, 1940–1945, le dernier combat de Léon Blum* (Paris: Robert Laffont, 2009), p. 75.

14. Édouard Daladier, *Journal de captivité, 1940–1945* (Paris: Calmann-Lévy, 1991), p. 74.

15. Quoted in Missika, *Je vous promets de revenir*, p. 86.

16. Birnbaum, *The Jews of the Republic*, chap. 22.

17. The official documents of the trial are in AN 570/19. On this judicial imbroglio, see Pierre Béteille and Christiane Rimbaud, *Le procès de Riom* (Paris: Plon, 1973), pp. 106 ff.

18. Léon Blum, "La prison et le procès," in *L'oeuvre de Léon Blum, 1940–1945*, pp. 194 ff.

19. Léon Blum, "À l'échelle humaine," in *L'oeuvre de Léon Blum, 1940–1945*, p. 409.

20. Quoted in Missika, *Je vous promets de revenir*, pp. 130–137.

21. AN 570 AP/19, file 3BL2Dr3.

22. Blum, "La prison et le procès," in *L'oeuvre de Léon Blum, 1940–1945*, p. 167.

23. His handwritten notes in preparation for his summation can be found in AN 570 AP/21, file 3BL5Dr2 to Dr6.

24. Ibid., p. 307.

25. *Le Petit Parisien*, March 12, 1942; *Le Cri du Peuple*, February 21 and March 11 and 12, 1942; *Au Pilori*, March 12, 1942; *Jeu-*

nesse, March 8, 1942; *L'Appel*, March 5, 1942; *Paris-Soir*, February 23, 1942. In October 1941, Jean Azéma called for "death for Daladier, death for Reynaud, death for the Jews Mandel and Blum"; *Le Cri du Peuple*, October 21, 1941; *Gringoire*, February 27, 1942. All of these articles can be found in AN F/7/15288.

26. Blum, "La prison et le procès," in *L'oeuvre de Léon Blum, 1940–1945*, p. 329.

27. For Tony Judt, "That he [Blum] was loyal to France is a tribute to the strength of his republican faith. For France was decidedly unloyal to him." Judt, *The Burden of Responsibility: Blum, Camus, Aron, and the French Twentieth Century* (Chicago: University of Chicago Press, 1998), p. 44.

28. Quoted in Henri Michel, *Le procès de Riom* (Paris: Albin Michel, 1979), pp. 320 ff.

29. Jules Blacas, *Sous l'étreinte juive* (Paris: Centre de documentation et de propagande, 1941), p. 81.

30. *L'Oeuvre*, March 14, 1942. AN F/7/15288.

31. Michel, *Le procès de Riom*, p. 107.

32. AN F/7/15288. "American journalists appeared to admire the way in which M. Léon Blum presented his defense." Report by the Renseignements Généraux dated February 19, 1943. This same carton in the archives also contains many clippings from the collaborationist press.

33. Michel, *Le procès de Riom*, p. 370.

34. AN 570 AP/19, file 3BL2Dr2.

35. Blum, "Le procès et la prison," in *L'oeuvre de Léon Blum, 1940–1945*, pp. 350, 358.

36. Ibid., p. 381.

37. AN 570 AP/19.

38. Ibid.

39. Marc Sadoun, *Les socialistes sous l'occupation* (Paris: Presses de la Fondation nationale des sciences politiques, 1982), pp. 185 ff.

40. Blum, "À l'échelle humaine," in *L'oeuvre de Léon Blum, 1940–1945*, p. 458.

41. Quoted in Missika, *Je vous promets de revenir*, pp. 198–199.

42. Ibid., p. 217.

43. A report indicated that a Provisional Administrator had inventoried the "belongings of the Jew Léon Blum. . . . It therefore remains for the Administrator to complete the dossier of the Jew Léon Blum" so that said belongings could be put up for sale on orders of the Commissariat Général aux Questions Juives. AN 570 AP/19, file 3BL1Dr3. Another report stated: "I have today had the opportunity to review the statement of the Jew Léon Blum." The sale of this "uncultivated land" was to take place on March 25, 1943, according to the public notice.

44. AN F/7/15288.

45. Quoted in Missika, *Je vous promets de revenir,* pp. 198–199.

46. AN 570 AP/19, file 3BL1Dr4. *Le Populaire* also wrote: "We turn to the people and say: Beware! To his torturers Léon Blum is merely a symbol on which they have focused all the hatred they feel toward you. And it is for you that he earned their hatred." In September 1943, the underground newspaper returned to the subject: "It is three years since Léon Blum was arrested by the French police. On this anniversary, our thoughts are with our courageous comrade, who, having courageously endured his own country's prisons, is now valiantly enduring his deportation to Germany."

47. Léon Blum, "Le dernier mois," in *L'oeuvre de Léon Blum, 1940–1945,* p. 517.

48. Quoted in Léon Blum, *Lettres de Buchenwald,* ed. Ilan Greilsammer (Paris: Gallimard, 2003), p. 37.

49. Ibid., p. 46.

50. For Jean Lacouture, Janot "hastened to place herself in the hands of the torturers in order to share the ordeal of the man who was the light of her life." Lacouture, *Une vie de rencontres* (Paris: Le Seuil, 2005), p. 225.

51. Quoted in Blum, *Lettres de Buchenwald,* ed. Greilsammer, p. 37.

52. Ibid., p. 130.

53. Ibid., p. 134.

54. APP, BA 1978.

55. Jorge Semprun, who was present at Buchenwald, described the scene in *Quel beau dimanche!* (Paris: Grasset, 1980), pp. 278 ff.

56. The original can be found in AN 570 AP/21, file 3BL6Dr2. An important part of this codicil in nearly the same wording appears in Blum, "Notes d'Allemagne," *L'oeuvre de Léon Blum, 1940–1945*, p. 513. On February 21, 1945, while still a prisoner, Blum "trembled" at the thought that the "cruelty" and "terror" unleashed by the Germans would be transmitted to those who opposed them in a spirit of revenge. This would be "to shape the world in your image, according to your laws, according to the Right of the Mighty. That would be your true victory. In a war of ideas, the winner is the party that inspires peace." Ibid. For Blum, the only solution was to integrate Germany into an international community. Blum, "À l'échelle humaine," in *L'oeuvre de Léon Blum, 1940–1945*, p. 479.

57. AN 570 AP/21. From his Buchenwald prison, Blum considered the Communist Party's claim to the "party of the martyred." He wrote: "Counting the number of party members shot by the enemy is not ipso facto proof that the party played a preponderant role in the Resistance. Counting the number of martyrs does not prove that the party supplied the majority of heroes. The Jews could make the same claim and formulate the same implicit demand. It would be no more justified if they did." AN 570 AP/21.

58. The original can be found in AN 570 AP/21, file 3BL6Dr2. See also Blum, "Notes d'Allemagne," pp. 512–513.

59. Letters of August 14 and September 20, 1944, quoted in Greilsammer, *Blum*, pp. 149, 158.

60. Blum, "Le dernier mois," in *L'oeuvre de Léon Blum, 1940–1945*, pp. 518–519. See also the similar account of his captivity and liberation that Blum published in *Le Populaire* on May 21, 23, 25, and 28, 1945.

61. Quoted in Missika, *Je vous promets de revenir*, p. 251.

62. AN 570 AP/21.

63. Blum, "Le dernier mois," in *L'oeuvre de Léon Blum, 1940–1945*, p. 533.

64. *Le Populaire*, May 15, 1945. On Blum's return, see AN 570 AP/22, file 4BL1Dr1.

65. These and many other letters can be found in AN 570 AP/22, file 4BL1Dr1.

66. Tereska Torrès subsequently published many books, including *Les années anglaises: Journal intime de guerre, 1939–1945* (Paris: Le Seuil, 1981), and *Une Française libre: Journal, 1939–1945* (Paris: Phebus, 2000).

67. Blum's notes can be found in AN 570 AP/22, file 4BL1Dr3.

68. These letters can be found in AN 570 AP/22, file 4BL1Dr2.

69. Robert Paxton, *Vichy France: Old Guard and New Order, 1940–1944* (New York: Columbia University Press, 1970).

Chapter 9. Kfar Blum

1. See the description in "Prospectus: Parents and Friends of Kfar Blum," Kfar Blum Kibbutz Archives. One kibbutznik wrote: "We are proud of Mr. Blum, but Mr. Blum and Jewry and progressive forces throughout the world may justly be proud of that small Jewish community which against all odds symbolized the right of the Jew to live and work and to die in the defense of this right." Engee Caller, "With Head Held High," *Furrows*, May 1946, p. 28.

2. *What the Founders Said: Addresses Delivered by Distinguished Statesmen and Leaders at the Founders' Dinner for the Leon Blum Colony in Palestine*, New York, p. 3. AN 570 AP/25, file 4BL6Dr2.

3. Birnbaum, *Les deux maisons*, pp. 269 ff.

4. Such as Sol Struck, the president of the American Jewish Committee, David Wertheim, secretary of Poale-Sion, Abraham Margulis of the Jewish National Workers' Alliance, Sol Low, president of the Federation of Galician Jews, and officials for the leading Jewish trade unions such as United Hebrew Trade. *What the Founders Said*, p. 5. Concerning this dinner and the plan to build the kibbutz, see Z. Alroy, "A Living Monument to Leon Blum in Galilee: The Story of How and Why the Leon Blum Colony Has Been Projected and Is Being Carried Forward to Successful Completion," Archives of the Kfar Blum Kibbutz. See also the description of the kibbutz with photos of Blum and pictures of fields and livestock in *Glimpses of Jewish Settlement History*, Youth Department, Keren Hayesod. The text reads: "Highly cultivated

and progressive, he [Blum] has fought gallantly to preserve human values. But he is also a Jew, and he has never turned his back on his own people. He is a warm friend of Zionism and an admirer of Jewish achievement in Palestine."

5. *What the Founders Said,* pp. 11–12.

6. Ibid., p. 27.

7. Ibid., p. 16.

8. Ibid., p. 17.

9. Moscow Archives, inventory 2, file 168.

10. Kfar Blum Kibbutz Archives. See also *La Terre retrouvée,* April 5, 1950.

11. Moshe Shertok Sharett, "A Great Man the Symbol," *Furrows,* November 1944, Kfar Blum Kibbutz Archives.

12. Kfar Blum Kibbutz Archives. See also Marc Jarblum, *Ils habiteront en sécurité: Du ghetto d'Europe à la Palestine* (Paris: Editions Réalité, 1947), p. 241. Since 1985 the kibbutz has sponsored a celebrated festival of classical music. Stanley Waterman, "Place, Culture, and Identity: Summer Music in Upper Galilee," *Transactions of the Institute of British Geographers,* vol. 23, 2001, p. 254.

13. After the rally Blum wrote to his wife Lise: "I was not unhappy about my Zionist rally last night, which was a very strange occasion." Moscow Archives, inventory 4, file 29.

14. *La Revue Juive,* March 15, 1925.

15. Moscow Archives, inventory 46, file 4–8.

16. Ibid., inventory 1, file 75.

17. Léon Blum, "Le devoir international vis-à-vis du Foyer national Juif," *Palestine,* March 1928, pp. 5, 11. Archives of the AIU, 4° U Br 1813.

18. *La terre retrouvée,* March 1930.

19. Marc Jarblum described this meeting in a little-known article, "Léon Blum, le sioniste," *Renaissance,* no. 3, October 1956.

20. Blumel, *Léon Blum, Juif et Sioniste,* p. 13.

21. Greilsammer, *Blum,* pp. 297 ff.

22. Ibid., p. 300.

23. Ibid., p. 302.

24. Blum, in *L'oeuvre de Léon Blum, 1945–1947,* p. 441.

25. See Greilsammer, *Blum*, p. 419, and François Lafon, *Pour une mise en perspective historique des relations entre la gauche française et le sionisme: L'exemple de Léon Blum et de son entourage jusqu'à la seconde guerre mondiale*, habilitation thesis, University of Paris 1, 2009, pp. 26, 299, 300.

26. Léon Blum, "Hommage à Weizmann," in *L'oeuvre de Léon Blum, 1947–1950*, p. 391. Oddly, most of the fundamental works on Weizmann say nothing at all about Blum. See, for example, Jehuda Reinharz, *Chaim Weizmann* (Oxford: Oxford University Press, 1985), and Thomas Fraser, *Chaim Weizmann: The Zionist Dream* (London: Haus, 2009).

27. Moscow Archives, inventory 1, file 243. French Judaism also thanked him for his support. For example, in January 1939, the Union des Sociétés OSE wrote: "We wish to express our gratitude for your kind attention and for the precious support you have given to our aid work." Moscow Archives, inventory 1, file 244.

28. Quoted in Birnbaum, *The Jews of the Republic*, p. 114.

29. Quoted in Michel Abitbol, *Les deux terres promises: Les Juifs de France et le sionisme* (Paris: Olivier Orban, 1989), p. 128.

30. Pierre Birnbaum, *"La France aux Français": Histoire des haines nationalistes* (Paris: Le Seuil, 1995), chap. 9.

31. Quoted in Abitbol, *Les deux terres promise*, p. 39.

32. As a socialist, Blum analyzed Arab-Jewish clashes in Palestine in terms of social class. In his view, "wealthy landowners looked on the new colonization with a fearful eye . . . [believing that it] would gradually destroy the old feudalism," whereas "the *fellahs*, the peasants, who have actually benefited from this Jewish colonization . . . had no interest in combating it." Quoted in Lafon, *Pour une mise en perspective historique des relations entre la gauche et le sionisme: L'exemple de Léon Blum et de son entourage jusqu'à la seconde guerre mondiale*, p. 232. Lafon quotes another little-known article by Blum in which he wrote: "It is indispensable and inevitable that the Arabs adapt better to Jewish immigration. If adaptation does not come from above, it will come from below. It is already happening. The humble Arab peasant is fraternizing with the humble Jewish peasant." Léon Blum, "Le Sionisme, la

Palestine et la vie socialiste," *Bulletin No. 9*, June 1935, quoted in Lafon, *Pour une mise*, p. 289.

33. Quoted in Abitbol, *Les deux terres promises*, p. 143.

34. Paula Hyman, *From Dreyfus to Vichy: The Remaking of French Jewry, 1906–1939* (New York: Columbia University Press, 1979), p. 263. On this point, see Catherine Nicault, "L'acculturation des israélites français au sionisme après la Grande Guerre," *Archives juives*, 2006/1, pp. 16 ff.

35. Antoine Compagnon, "Israël avant Israël," in *Les intellectuels français et Israël*, ed. Denis Charbit (Paris: Editions de l'Eclat, 2009), p. 24.

36. Edmond Fleg, *Pourquoi je suis juif?* (Paris: Les belles lettres, 1995), p. 50.

37. André Spire, *Souvenirs à bâtons rompus* (Paris: Albin Michel, 1962), p. 101. See Pierre Birnbaum, "D'un État à l'autre? L'impossible passage du franco-judaïsme au sionisme," in *Les intellectuels français et Israël*, ed. Charbit, p. 35.

38. Catherine Nicault, *La France et le sionisme, 1887–1948: Une rencontre manquée?* (Paris: Calmann-Lévy, 1992), p. 23.

39. Quoted in Lafon, *Pour une mise en perspective historique*, p. 162. In 1903, in his critique of Maurice Donnay's play "Le retour de Jérusalem," Blum defined Zionists as "Jews who would like to bring their co-religionists, now dispersed throughout the world, together in a homogeneous state around their traditional capital. For them, Zion is the true 'homeland.'" See *L'oeuvre de Léon Blum, 1891–1905*, pp. 205 ff. Blum was already defining Zionism in a way that placed greater stress on the state than on culture, but at that time he did not identify with it.

40. Quoted in Birnbaum, *Les deux maisons*, pp. 279, 280. It is easy to see why Sylvain Lévi condemned Brandeis's view and fought American Judaism, which he thought likely to encourage a kind of communitarianism incompatible with the French idea of public space.

41. Haïm Weizmann, *Naissance d'Israël* (Paris: Gallimard, 1957), p. 330.

42. *Notre Parole*, November 22, 1945.

43. AN 570 AP/25, file 4BL6Dr2.

44. Philippe Moine, *Les socialistes français devant le mouvement sioniste et la création de l'État d'Israël, 1945–1949*, DEA thesis, Institut d'études politiques, Paris, 1993, p. 93.

45. AN 570 AP/25, file 4BL6Dr2.

46. Ibid.

47. *Le Populaire*, July 6, 1946.

48. *Le Populaire*, August 21, 1946.

49. APP, BA 1978.

50. Idith Zertal, *Des rescapés pour un État: La politique sioniste d'immigration clandestine en Palestine, 1945–1949* (Paris: Calmann-Lévy, 2000), p. 74. A few weeks later, in dealing with the Quai d'Orsay, which was doing everything in its power to prevent these immigrants from coming, André Blumel, who had been named chief of staff to interior minister Adrien Tixier, reminded the new Socialist prime minister Paul Ramadier of Blum's position and asked him to require the civil servants at the Quai to do as Blum had directed.

51. AN 570 AP/25, file 4BL6Dr2.

52. These three texts by Blum on the *Exodus* can be found in Zertal, *Des rescapés*, pp. 74 ff.

53. Quoted in Tsilla Hershco, *Entre Paris et Jérusalem: La France, le sionisme et la création de l'État d'Israël* (Paris: Honoré Champion, 2003), p. 89.

54. I thank Claude Klein for this information.

55. AN 570 AP/25, file 4BL6Dr2.

56. Vincent Auriol, *Journal, 1947* (Paris: Armand Colin, 1970), p. 810.

57. Meanwhile, *La Terre Retrouvée*, February 1, 1947, claimed that Blum was acting solely as a French patriot. A curious incident took place in May 1962. During a debate organized by the Zionist Federation of France, André Memmi attacked Léon Blum as a "self-hating Jew." André Blumel immediately resigned. The president of the Federation sent him a letter of apology, stressing that "Léon Blum demonstrated his Judaism actively and positively by taking part in the difficult negotiations conducted by Weizmann,

and he was a member of the Jewish Agency from the time it was constituted." André Blumel Archives, Office Universitaire de Recherche Socialiste (OURS), 4 AP05. In 1965, when Blumel ran in Paris on the Union Démocratique ticket, he addressed "Jewish voters" and alluded to his action with Léon Blum. André Blumel Archives, OURS, 4 AP05.

58. APP, BA 1978.

59. David Lazar, *L'opinion française et la naissance de l'État d'Israël, 1945–1949* (Paris: Calmann-Lévy, 1972), p. 158.

60. Benjamin Pinkus, "Ben-Gurion, la France et les Juifs de France," in *Les Juifs de France, le sionisme et l'État d'Israël*, ed. Doris Bensimon and Benjamin Pinkus (Paris: Publications Langues O, 1989), p. 281.

61. David Ben Gourion, *Journal, 1947–1948* (Paris: Editions de La Martinière, 2012), p. 551.

Conclusion

1. The American and Canadian press greeted Blum's mission warmly. AN 570 AP/22, file 4BL2Dr1 to Dr3.

2. Both Roger Martin du Gard and Saint-John Perse used the word "sacrifice" in their letters. AN 570 AP/23. "Stay well," Perse added. "For you, too, it is a duty."

3. Léon Blum, "La question de Jérusalem," *Sion*, April 1950.

4. At the time he wrote: "As a socialist and, as I can say to you, also as a Jew, a collaboration with *Forward* is the solution that would be most satisfactory to me." Moscow Archives, inventory 2, file 8.

5. *L'oeuvre de Léon Blum, 1947–1950*, pp. 308 ff. This article was written in October 1949. Earlier, in January 1939, Blum said to the Chamber of Deputies: "We do not accept the reverse racism that would treat the Germans as a people incapable of climbing to the highest peaks of culture. . . . Our concern with national dignity and pride, our determination to block the designs of the fascists, will never lead us to overstatements of that kind." *Le Populaire*, January 27, 1939.

6. *Le Populaire*, April 3, 1950. One can consult any number of

documents that set forth the organization of the ceremony in minute detail. AN 570 AP/29 and 570 AP/30. The latter carton contains an impressive collection of clippings from the local, national, and international press. Among the guests were representatives of Poale Zion, the Mapam, and the Bund.

7. See *L'Humanité*, March 31, 1950.

8. AN 570 AP/30 contains a handwritten letter from Gide to Janot: "To my great regret, I could not be with you on January 8, much as I would have liked to join Léon's other friends, especially after hearing from you about the particularly warm sentiments toward me to the very end, which moved me deeply."

9. All these telegrams and many others can be found in AN 570 AP/29.

10. See the letter from André Malraux to Janot, AN 570 AP/30, file 5BL2Dr5: "Rest assured that you will always find my staff ready to help preserve the memory of Léon Blum as he deserves and to assist you in your endeavors to that end."

11. Bulletin du Conseil municipal de Paris, December 18, 1956, AN 570 AP/30.

12. AN 570 AP/30, file 5BL2Dr3. The judgment of February 14, 1962, contains the following passage: "Whereas the mention attached to the name of Léon Blum was a partial and approximate reproduction of a charge against a political man by polemicists who exceeded the proper bounds of political debate . . . [and] this slander was repeated between 1940 and 1945 when Léon Blum was prosecuted and then deported by the enemy occupying French territory," the court "declares and judges that by designating André Léon Blum by the words 'Blum (Léon Karfulkenstein),' Éditions Larousse has committed a culpable error."

13. Pierre Birnbaum, "La valse des statues," *L'Arche*, November 1985.

INDEX

JEWISH LIVES is a major series of interpretive
biography designed to illuminate the imprint of Jewish
figures upon literature, religion, philosophy, politics, cultural
and economic life, and the arts and sciences. Subjects are
paired with authors to elicit lively, deeply informed books that
explore the range and depth of Jewish experience
from antiquity through the present.

Jewish Lives is a partnership of Yale University Press
and the Leon D. Black Foundation.

Ileene Smith is editorial director. Anita Shapira and
Steven J. Zipperstein are series editors.